The Rusty Nut Bible

How to Undo Seized,
Damaged or Broken Nuts,
Bolts, Studs & Screws

By

Chas Newport

---

* The Rusty Nut Bible EN-UK v4.2

ACKNOWLEDGMENTS

References to all brand names and trademarks are mentioned under the principle of nominative fair use. I'm not a representative of any brands except NRTFM.com, my publishing company. None of my opinions have been paid for in cash, freebies or other favours.

Intentionally Blank

TRIPLE-JUMP INDEX

INTRODUCTION

There had been much swearing. Now, a small amount of blood oozed from my knuckles. I felt the pressure. The car would lose a huge chunk of its value with a seized brake. We couldn't afford a tow-truck or a big labour bill.

Two opposing corners of the hex head left intact. The damaged ones were important. But I couldn't read the signs. One chance left...

Blowtorch: impossible. Brake hoses, ABS wires, and the fuel tank. Space: too cramped to grind, saw or file the damaged bolt head off. And trying to extract a headless stump didn't seem like progress. It needed to be undone using the head and the thread.

Necessity is the mother of invention and the grandmother of a trillion Google searches. After sifting through many bits of good but unusable advice, I found my answer; I used a freeze spray. It worked like a charm, shrinking the bolt, seeping into the gap that created. The relief and elation of that success inspired the first draft of this book. Everything I discovered is here. Myths are in the bin, and solutions ranked in order of aggression.

Starting with less aggression has bonuses. Basic tools you are likely to own, cheap consumables. Reduced collateral damage to valuable parts, and less risk of injury. Since that first draft, I've added dozens of new hints, tips, tools and deeper information on fasteners, metallurgy and mechanics.

*Once you understand, you don't
need to remember.*

Conventions

A few things before we start.

None of the brands I use are direct sponsors, paying me to mention them. All tools, accessories and consumables are purchased by me, or with my publishing company's money. This avoids any accusations of bias or favouritism. Links on our website pay us a small commission paid by the seller.

This book is in UK English:

Sceptical of his innocence, they analysed the coloured aluminium disc to mount a defence of his behaviour.

In a few places, we've repeated information, so you don't have to flick back and forth. We will repeat warnings in situ, in case you dip in from the Triple Jump Index during a job.

When I mention "we" in the body of the book, I'm talking with you. Here, I'm referring to myself and my wife, Sooz. She works two jobs, devoting her weekends to proofreading, photography and building web pages. When you re-read your own writing, you recall what you wrote, often missing your own mistakes. Without her fresh eyes, there would be many mistakes. There may still be a few. But we've both worked hard to make a high-quality product. Nobody's perfect. If you find any problems we missed, please get in touch. You can contact us at *ⱡhttps://nrtfm.com* or *ⱡhttps://therustynutbible.com*.

A dagger † shown in text or under a picture is an external link. Print readers can use these too by browsing: *†https://therustynutbible.com/ links. Links have further information or products on our website.*

Safety

The last point before we start is safety. People mock health and safety as bureaucratic and weak, but I don't think that's right. You require discipline, patience and the nerve to stop while under pressure from time or expectations. A friend of mine watched a man die before the ambulance arrived, because he didn't attach his safety-harness to the static line. I learnt from that, we all should.

Intentionally Blank

COMMON KNOWLEDGE

This is one of those subjects where solutions are "common knowledge." But popularity and repetition don't mean something is the best right or even right, it just means people think it is.

It isn't true shaving makes hair thicker or its growth faster. The illusion occurs because a day of growth is a greater proportion of a short hair and shows more against bare skin

It isn't true fingernails and hair grow after you die. The grisly truth is, that you dehydrate and your skin shrinks away from them.

It isn't true we don't use 100% of our brain, we use all of it for various tasks and activities. We just don't use the whole thing at the same time.

Visual Index

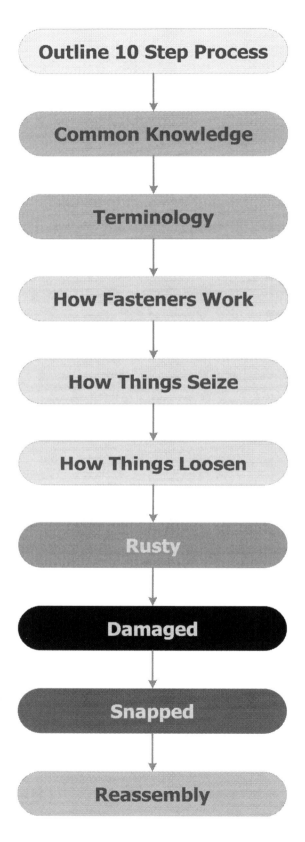

- Outline 10 Step Process
- Common Knowledge
- Terminology
- How Fasteners Work
- How Things Seize
- How Things Loosen
- Rusty
- Damaged
- Snapped
- Reassembly

Not Solutions

The common knowledge solutions for rusty fasteners are often not solutions at all, but impatient shortcuts. Shortcuts with a higher chance of failure than a more restrained approach. All involve brute force and heat.

Collateral damage possibilities are everywhere. Painted parts have many layers of inhibitor, primer, undercoat, paint and lacquer. You may even have rubber, plastic or composites nearby. Vehicles have hoses, wiring, sensors and chips in everything.

Use Brute Force

Internet nugget one is just to increase leverage until it moves. More torque force only requires a longer lever or a heavy friend. Sometimes the bolt snaps and the tools go clattering to the floor and you or your heavy friend get hurt. If it snaps flush you have a stump in a hole. For a protruding stump it might not come off the remains of the shaft, hindered by adjacent parts. With that blocking you, you may struggle for access to cut the rest of it. You're in real trouble...

Grind It Off

Internet nugget two is to grind off the fastener head. But a large diameter spinning disc is not a scalpel. Even when access lets you use something this big, you'll leave a mark here and there. With my brake calliper, bolt-head removal was a non-starter. I had no room for a saw or grinder, plus brake hoses I couldn't move because of a lack of slack.

And it suffers all the same problems as brute force with a protruding stump.

Heat It Up

Internet nugget three is to heat the fastener you are struggling to extract. It must glow cherry red, as no other shade of fruit will do, apparently. This is the ultimate illustration of Internet wisdom because it has a grain of truth at the core, it actually works well for a nut on a bolt with good access.

But a bolt is not an expandable ring, it's an enclosed cylinder. Expanded, the bolt is wider than the hole, making it tighter. To release pressure, you must make the hole wider, so you need to warm the surrounding metal. The large mass acts as a heat-sink, conducting it away from the point you are warming. In my example, that's partly what a brake calliper does... dissipate heat soak from the disc and pads to stop the brake fluid boiling.

My brake calliper presented other difficulties. In a car the rustiest components are underneath, but fragile objects share that space. Brake hoses, bushes, and wiring for sensors in ABS and traction control appear here at the places they attach.

Heating an enclosed bolt can bring benefits after it cools. The expansion and contraction cycle may help crack the rust and dirt bonding the head and upper part of the thread. But it's still risky. The ten steps below have six highly effective, complementary actions to try before we resort to that level of risk. Parts of my brake calliper came free at steps 4 and 6. No flames, no collateral damage, no bleeding.

THE TEN STEP PROCESS

Here's an outline of the ten-step sequence you can download as a sample without buying the complete book:

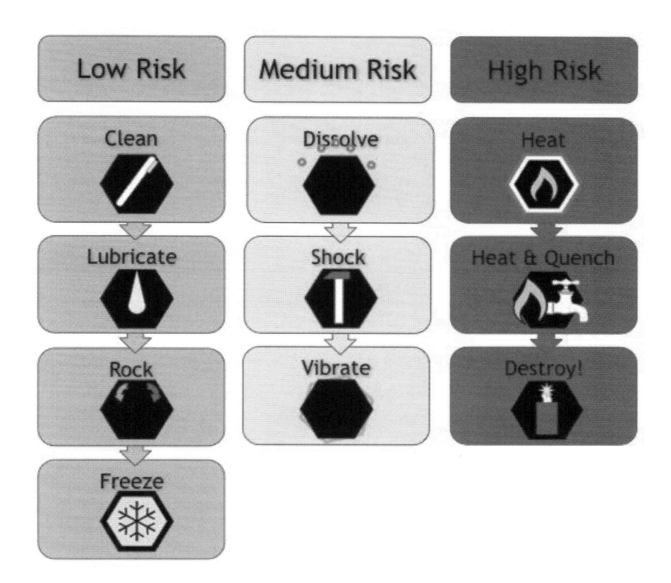

We wish you the best of luck and a safe solution to your problem. If you want additional help, here's a summary of the details in rest of the book.

For each of the ten steps, we give more detail on how and why it works. Knowing why is important for two reasons. First, you don't have to remember things you understand. Second, understanding let's you create new solutions of your own.

We'll highlight how the order of the steps works as compound interest, each building on the ones before it, and when to repeat them to multiply effectiveness.

If things are worse than a seized fastener, or a breakage occurs during the steps, we've got you covered. Here's a list of step-by-step guides:

- Dealing with damaged heads.
- Dealing with damaged nuts.
- Repairing damaged threads.
- Replacing damaged threads.
- Extracting sheared shafts.
- Smart reassembly.

There are extensive appendices on:

- Useful tools and gadgets.
- Lubricants and consumables.
- Personal protective equipment (PPE).
- The Six Simple Machines (plus Hydraulics).

TERMINOLOGY

Fastening items into assemblies was born the moment someone lashed a stone on a stick to bash something harder. The leap to attaching a flint on a long pole or handle was a game changer for our entire species.

Even something as complex as a helix wrapped around a shaft dates back farther than you might guess. It pre-dates fasteners by over a thousand years. The 3rd century BCE saw the invention of efficient helical pumps called Archimedes, or Egyptian, screws. Helical threads used to exert pressure date back to the 4th, in presses for olives and grapes. The fastener on a thread, assembling parts was not thought of until the 1400s.

Threads

We classify threads by the direction to **tighten.** When the head is facing you right-hand threads tighten clockwise, left-hand threads tighten anticlockwise. Use the phrase "Lefty-loosey, righty-tighty," to recall how to turn a right-handed thread. Position or imagine the tool in a vertical position, push the top left or right.

Most fasteners are right-handed. My 90s 4x4 only has one reverse thread, the nut which holds the cooling fan. The left pedal on every bike is a left-hand thread, so peddling doesn't unscrew it. They are rare, but worth looking for. Your fastener may not be seized... you might be tightening it. Don't worry, I won't say a word [walks away whistling].

Threads are internal or external**. *Internal*-**threads are inside a fastener, or ***tapped*** into a part, ***external*-**threads around a shaft. The thread and fastener will always match in the direction they tighten.

Over time, conventions emerged among small groups within industries or small areas. Some developed, while others dropped out of use but were not dropped by everyone. Throw in regional and national variation and things become even more confusing.

Trivia:

*The Industrial Revolution changed everything, so most changes in threading fasteners are within the last 150 years. Prior to 1841, no standard dimensions prevailed for threads, except those adopted by individual manufacturers. They did it for their own catalogues, usually within niche activities. Observing the issue (Sir) Joseph Whitworth invented the first national thread definition, which later became a **†British Standard (BSW)**.*

His system starts with the ***pitch***, the distance the shaft moves in or out in a single turn. Thread angle does not determine the pitch of the thread, it is the distance between the ridges of the helix. When close, we call them fine, wider ones are coarse. First, Whitworth set his thread slope at 55 degrees, calculating depth and radius as fractions of the pitch. Then he defined a table of pitches, based on shaft diameter, to create a complete array of sizes. This standardisation allowed bulk manufacture, with reliable storage and supply chains between many industries.

Fastener & Shaft

Despite this book's title, a seized nut on a shaft isn't our only scenario. With my brake calliper, the first bolt was stuck in a tapped hole in another part I couldn't move or access easily, which is pretty common. The second was threaded through a tube, but water had got inside and rusted it along the entire length.

Panels with attachments often use a *†captive nut, caged* or welded on the other side. They are put there before assembly and often enclosed or inaccessible afterwards. Items added after assembly may use a *†rivet nut or rivnut*, a rivet with a thread inside. These can be inserted blind, without access to the other side.

We can't mention every one of these each time we explain a step. For simplicity and clarity we need a generic set of terms. So, the item at the other end, whether it's a part with a thread or some kind of nut, is the ***fastener.***

The bolt, stud, threaded bar, or screw thread is the ***shaft***. When forming a ***bolted joint***, the shaft and fastener make a ***fastening***.

Shaft & Head

Views abound on the distinction between a bolt and a **screw**. We need not embroil ourselves in that. A screw is just a shaft with a **head** at one end, and an external thread which creates (self-taps) an internal thread when turned. We will use the term **bolt** for any shaft with a head on one end unless the tool is specifically for screws. It's shorthand and it's the most common thing you'll want to loosen.

A head is really just a shape, and so is a nut. It doesn't matter if we turn it or hold still with a tool. Where a technique is equally applicable to a bolt head, screw head, or nut we'll just say *head*.

External Drive

Externally driven heads start with straight sided shapes like the wing nut, triangle, square, and hexagon. Bi-hexagon (bi-hex) is what you'd imagine from the name... two hexagons offset by thirty degrees. The twelve corners make engaging easier and distribute force over more contact points. There are also many proprietary designs.

They maximise size and leverage for a shaft and are more sturdy than internal drives. But they need to be, because people use ill-fitting open ended spanners, loading force onto two corners of a hexagonal head. In the past, I've been using metric spanners on cars while unaware they used other systems. Equivalent sizes can be visually so close, you don't realise.

They don't trap dirt or water like a head with a hole. Steel ones rust but hold their shape because they weather more evenly, and dry out faster. The biggest plus is availability of **Adjustable** & **Wall Drive** spanners.

The only con for an external-drive is that it's surfaces are exposed to physical wear-and-tear, which weaken it and might reduce it to a non-standard size. Fear not, we have ways of making them torque!

Internal Drive

Internally driven heads engage via a drive-hole or slot into which a tool of the same shape and size fits. The simplest are the straight or star shaped slots used on old-school wood-screws, others are simple geometrical shapes, such as triangles, squares and hexagons (aka Allen). There is a vast variety of proprietary stars, slots, lobes and splines (ribs).

Internal is better than external because force is evenly distributed to every contact point of the opening. However, some openings are bevelled, some are vertical. The latter are favoured in precision engineering because they don't jump out.

Drive-holes need a thick sidewall for strength, that means bits are thinner than an equal width of external drive. Flutes and splines on the bit can make them weak because the core is thin. If you don't use high quality bits, they'll break before the head moves. This often damages the innards of the head as they smear across it. If magnetised they leave splinters in the hole.

While we're discussing fragments, general contamination can be an issue. Dirt can get into the drive opening and, sheltered now, it won't self clean. It's tough to see and difficult to remove.

Weather erosion is worse because water gathers in the drive-hole and holds there by surface tension. The smaller relative size means it has a relatively larger effect, in proportion to the original size of the opening.

Internal drive bits don't have an equivalent of a spanner. There are socket bits but you can't always apply pressure when you turn them from the side if space is tight. Not an issue if the assembly allows access for maintenance as it should, but modern cars pack many items into cramped spaces. If they assemble in a specific order on a production line, parts may obscure the fastening.

Trivia:

Our car with the brake calliper problem needed the front bumper off to change the sidelight bulbs! That was because the Xenon headlights were added to the design late and were bigger than the old halogens.

Hex Is King

Except for tool choice, the *drive* doesn't influence our ***ten steps.*** First, because hex-heads are, by far, the most commonplace in DIY. Second, the tool is either an opening on a ***Lever*** or the shaped end of a lever or rigid ***Wheel & Axle***. If calling a screwdriver a wheel and axle sounds odd, please see ***Appendix D: The Six Simple Machines***.

The dominance and long history of externally driven hex-heads is a boon for us, because we can use a small set of basic tools. The better news is, the many special tools for hex-heads; from alternate drive systems like pass-through and wall/surface drive to self adjusting grippers which tighten as you turn them. Ultra fine ratchets, crescent ratchets and dozens of odd necks, gimbals, shafts and handles for awkward angles, all make our task easier. There is far less choice for other head configurations.

If you're intrigued look in *Appendix A: The Right Tools for the Job on page 128*

Summary

I realise we covered a lot of ground there, so let's summarise our terms:

◆ Bolt, stud, threaded bar (Allthread®) or screw shafts are all *shafts*.

◆ Thread around a shaft: *external*.

◆ Thread in a hole: *internal*.

◆ Nut, captive nut, rivnut or tapped hole: *fastener*.

◆ Anything we apply a tool to: *head*.

◆ Bolt or screw, a shaft with a head: *bolt*.

◆ Posidriv, Allen, Torx, etc: *internally driven heads*.

◆ Square, hex, bi-hex, etc: *externally driven heads*.

◆ Bolt and fastener: *fastening*.

◆ Fastening and parts: *assembly*.

◆ Multiple assemblies: *structure*.

Intentionally Blank

HOW FASTENERS WORK

To understand how joints seize we should understand how they work before rust enters the equation.

If you aren't interested in this this, skip to *How Things Seize on page 41*

Elastic .vs. Plastic Deformation

Threaded fasteners work on tension. Imagine the helix of thread without the shaft in the middle, and it resembles a coiled spring. Holding a small pen spring in your hands, you can compress it or pull it and it works either way, up to a point. Pull too hard and the spring stays stretched. That is the change from elastic to inelastic deformation.

Elastic deformation stretches or compresses an object, after which it returns to its original length, depth or shape. The load below which this happens is the *elastic limit or yield point*. Plastic deformation happens for two reasons, the material isn't elastic, or we've stressed it past its limit. Markings on high quality fasteners tell us how how far we can stretch them before they reach that yield point.

The Bolted Joint

A shaft penetrates one or more components squeezing them together. The force *along* the axis of the bolt is the *clamp load or pre-load*. In engineering the resulting structure is the *bolted joint*. The underside of the shaft head and fastener (if used) are the *bearing surfaces*.

We can divide tightening into four distinct phases:

Run Down : where nothing is touching, we're taking up slack. A typical nut-and-bolt fastener should tighten with finger effort during run down. Check the thread for damage if it stops part way. Otherwise, clean both threads, then lubricate or re-apply thread-lock if needed.

Draw Down : closes all remaining gaps so there's contact between components, fastening and bearing surfaces. You need to pay attention to alignment in this phase.

Elastic Deformation : adds torque, so clamped parts compress, the shaft stretches and pre-load is set. Correct torque is enough for security, without the fastener failing. We call this *pre-load* to distinguish it from the external static load caused by gravity or dynamic forces applied to it.

The pre-load of bolted joints should use only 85-95 percent of the yield strength. This value is called *proof load* because it's a margin for error below which it should always be safe.

Plastic Deformation : should never happen, components and/or shaft irreparably damaged. Any sudden fall off in the force you feel from a tool, other than a torque wrench, is the thread stripping or the fastener exceeding the yield strength. You should dispose of the entire fastening.

Tension .vs. Friction

Tension and friction correlate, and as you'd expect there's an equation... the good news for those of you who hate maths is, we're only concerned with one symbol.

$$\textit{Imperial version: } T = (DPK)/12$$

T = Torque in lbft (ftlbs in the US)
D = Nominal diameter in inches (hence the division by 12)
P = Desired tension or clamp load in lbs.

$$\textit{Metric version: } T = (DPK)/1000$$

T in Nm
D in mm (hence the division by 1000)
P in Newtons.

In both formulas the letter "*K*" is the term of most importance to us. It is the *coefficient of friction*. It measures how easily the surfaces slide over each other. In clean joints it affects the losses from pre-load, in rusty ones it greatly increase, seizing the fastener in position. The trouble is, *K* changes through several hard to measure factors:

◆ Surface Texture
◆ Fastener Materials
◆ Lubricant Quality and Quantity
◆ Humidity
◆ Debris

- ◆ Rust
- ◆ Type of Thread and Machining
- ◆ Other Environmental Factors

With all this affecting pre-load, torque controlled fastenings can be unpredictable. This creates underloaded joints which loosen, and overloaded ones which break. Most industries quote torque values based on a dry fastening, which is odd because they jump and stick more than lubricated ones. That adds even more inconsistency.

This has been addressed by the invention of swaged fasteners, but they need bulky, expensive, specialised tools. Those powered guns apply direct, measured tension to the shaft, then squeeze a collar on at an exact, consistent value set by the operator. They cannot slacken and liquid is excluded, because they need no clearance for the fastener to turn. Used in places where access is difficult, for instance, sub-sea applications or wind turbines, these are outside our scope for this book. Most fasteners we come across will be torque-controlled.

Friction Fastening

In friction-only joints the tension creates friction between the assembled surfaces:

- ◆ Head bearing surface to washer or top part.
- ◆ Each washer and part to the adjacent part.
- ◆ Surfaces of internal and external threads.
- ◆ Bottom part surface to bearing surface of fastener.

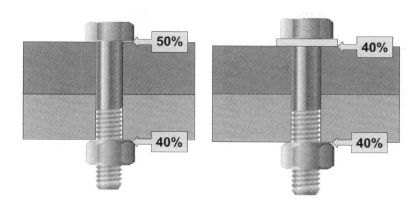

Figure 1 Friction Losses

Up to 90 percent of the applied torque can be lost at the two bearing surfaces, less with washers. The principal purpose of *plain* washers is to be hard and smooth, cutting the value of *K*. The aim is to reduce losses at the bearing surfaces, passing more pre-load into the shaft. Plain washers also pass less force back to the fastener to cause loosening, but moving joints still use targeted friction enhancers.

Friction Enhancers

Friction enhancers *should* prevent items loosening once tightened. A range of techniques are used to lock fasteners in position or increase friction between the fastener, the thread and the outer parts.

Lock Nuts : are pairs of nuts locked against one another, binding the thread. They jam against each other, raising friction on a localised portion of thread and the bearing faces of the adjacent nuts.

Nylon Locking Nuts : have inserts designed to increase friction with the thread. You can't tighten them by hand once the friction enhancer meets the thread. We use most "dry" as lubrication would defeat the purpose of the device. Check the manufacturer's directions for details.

<u>WARNING:Temperature</u>

Check for temperature limits as synthetic thermoplastics will melt beyond at approximately 250 °F (121 °C).

Thread-lock Adhesives : start out thin and flowing, but set like flexible glue to suppress spontaneous movement. They are engineered to break under high load for disassembly. They blend them for various torque ranges, heat resistance and to specifically exclude moisture from the thread.

As with the enhanced friction nuts, this method means you can't use a traditional lubricant. But, applied and tightened before it cures, the thread-lock should act as the lube, preventing torque jumps.

This does not apply to the factory applied "patch lock" you see in a coloured band around bolts used in brake callipers and other high-vibration applications. That will increase effort during all phases of tightening. You should not reuse this type of fastening and they are usually supplied with the parts you are fitting.

Friction washers act at the bearing surfaces of the head and the fastener. There are dozens of configurations from a single offset split, to dozens of tiny spring loaded wings. The idea is to prevent loosening by vibration. They make most from hard, but elastic (springy), materials to dig into the assembled parts for grip and absorb vibration.

High quality is essential, or they will suffer plastic deformation, flatten and do nothing. There are many videos showing these being tried on a _†Junker rig_, very few do as intended in this test.

Tension Fastening

†Nord-Lock® (_†HEICO-Lock_® in the UK) has designed a system to prevent assemblies vibrating apart. Wedge-lock washers form a mechanical linkage with the bearing surfaces, exploiting the tension and elasticity we explained earlier.

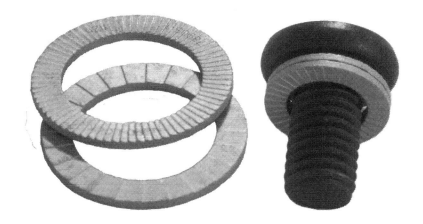

Figure 2 Nord-Lock Washers

Wedge-locks are a two part hardened washer with radial gripping ribs on the outside and wedge shaped ramps (or cams) inside. Note that the ramps must be steeper than the angle of the thread, so take care to buy the correct one for the fastener in use.

The washers must be harder than the fastener and bearing surfaces of the assembly. The ribs bite into them making a mechanical, not frictional, connection. You must be alert to fakes. From 2011 they have the brand name for verification and a code showing what the material is, so you can check relative hardness. Here's a table of the codes for reference.

Washer type	Code
Steel washers, Delta Protekt® coating	flZn
Stainless steel washers	SS
254 SMO®	254
INCONEL® / HASTELLOY® C-276	276
INCONEL® 718	718

Tightening a wedge-lock, the vertical faces of the ramps interlock, both halves move as one. It's like a one-piece, ribbed anti-friction washer but is not spring loaded. The hardened outer ribs bite into the head, fastener and bearing surfaces. This creates a solid 2-dimensional connection along the shaft. These washers do leave permanent marks in the surface material or finish.

Remember, the internal ramps are steeper than the thread angle. When loosening, the half by the head or fastener must climb the one on the bearing surface. This only happens if the shaft stretches. Applied and tightened as directed, it can't occur spontaneously, you must apply a torsional force with a lever to stretch the bolt.

This **wedge-lock** fastening system uses a lubricated shaft and fastener. Dry threads jump, making correct torque setting difficult. Lubrication reduces frictional losses at the thread interface, stops the jumping and helps transfer torque to the shaft. They also suggest a *greater* torque value than you use for dry threads, which may mean using a stronger class of bolt. This might not work if parts of the bolted joint are too soft. Refer to the manufacturer's website and product leaflets for details and the X Series washer description below.

WARNING: Tell Others

If you switch to these washers, make sure others working on it know. They do come apart at disassembly and the correct orientation of the ramps on the two halves isn't obvious, nor is the fact they are a matched pair. Through-bolted parts require one either side. If they expect that shaft to be dry, they may apply thread-lock which won't work without degreasing. As use of them becomes more widespread, the information should spread.

X-Series

The only flaw in the original Wedge Lock design was loss of tension over the long term, which can happen for several reasons we'll cover in *How Things Loosen*.

Their X-Series washers address this with built-in expansion ring. This allows compression of layers and relaxation in the shaft, with less loss of pre-load.

Intentionally Blank

HOW THINGS SEIZE

If you already know about this you can skip to *How Things Loosen on page 45*

Rusting

Rusting refers specifically to the oxidation of iron (Fe) to Iron (III) Oxide. It probably gets a word to itself through shear abundance, making up a third of the Earth's crust. If you consider oxides, hydroxides, and oxyhydroxides there are sixteen oxygen bearing compounds of iron. The inhabitants of colder climes have an astonishing number of words for snow, it's surprising we only have one word for rust!

Metals exposed to dry air at atmospheric pressure don't oxidise, that's why they have those vast aircraft and vehicle graveyards in places like Nevada. In temperate regions air isn't dry and the water acts as a catalyst for the reaction we call rusting.

Corrosion

Often used as a synonym for rust, corrosion refers to a **loss** of material and has its root in a Latin word for *gnawing*. Seen in non-ferrous metals, like aluminium, it can still cause problems if the material carried away dries out or reacts to form a crystalline compound in a thread. It happens via several mechanisms.

Physical Erosion : is a simple physical effect like liquid sandpaper. Atmospheric water contains dust, sand and other airborne particles which physically wear the material, lifting particles into suspension.

Chemical Erosion : happens when the metal forms a compound which dissolves in water to make a solution. Atmospheric water often contains dissolved oxygen and other chemicals which react with metals. Cold water can sustain a higher oxygen saturation than warm water.

Electrolysis : is like chemical erosion but the mechanism is the movement of charged metal ions through a liquid. We power this process with batteries to plate things with chromium, vanadium and other hard coatings. Ironically we also use it to anodise aluminium with inert anti-corrosion coatings.

Electrolysis can occur spontaneously at all mixed-metal interfaces if the correct electrolyte is present, creating a low-voltage battery. It can sometimes occur with non-metals like carbon or lasagne...

Science Bit:

The lasagne cell occurs when you cook food in a steel baking tray. After cooking someone places aluminium foil over, to keep it moist and protected. But the acid in tomatoes acts as an electrolyte. If the lasagne sauce touches the foil it only takes a few hours for patches of aluminium to migrate into it. Small contact areas will make holes.

Steel and aluminium (Al) are often used adjacent to each other for a combination of strength and lightness. The combination is common in engines where the block and head use aluminium but bolts, studs and nuts are steel.

Trivia:

Luigi Galvani is famous for his discovery that frogs legs twitch when touched with metal surgical tools. The phenomenon is called Galvanism or Galvanisation in his honour. He believed it was "animal electricity" stored in the muscle. This spawned (Sorry ... I'm not really!) the phrase "galvanised into action". The reference to zinc plated metal as "galvanised" came via French, again as a nod to Galvani.

Friction

Seized fastenings get that way via the processes described above. They change the surface of the fastener and the shaft making them pitted and rough. The compounds are coarse and gritty further increasing friction between the roughened surfaces.

From this point we will only use the term rust. The products of corrosion and electrolysis have similar characteristics and will respond to the same techniques.

Cement

These compounds, by definition, integrate additional atoms which add mass and increase the size of the resulting compound. Crystalline compounds often align into a three-dimensional grid with larger gaps between the molecules. That makes the compounds bulkier then the pure elemental metal. This fills the tiny clearance gap in the thread like cement and can be remarkably strong. The roughened surfaces act as a "key" causing the cement to adhere stubbornly to them.

> **Brittle = Breakable:** *Luckily crystals have an inherent weakness, their structure is **brittle**: 1. hard but liable to break easily.*

> *Synonyms: breakable, splintery, fragile, frail, delicate, frangible; rigid, hard, crisp.*

As you'll see in the next section, this brittleness is the key to solving the problem of a seized fastener. Brittle materials are strong against gradually applied forces but vulnerable to impact, vibration and rapid temperature changes. We will exploit this in an ordered approach minimising injury risk and collateral damage.

HOW THINGS LOOSEN

If you're impatient for getting the job done go to ***Rusty on page 49***

Many of the same things which will loosen a joint we don't want loosened, have a similar effect on a rusty one gummed up with crystalline compounds.

Vibration

Vibration deserves a special mention because it's the biggest factor in dynamic loosening. It's particularly severe on brake, suspension and engine components in bikes, cars, boats, trains and planes. Fasteners in these systems are often on pivot points, which means they are subject to both linear and rotational forces.

Rotational (axial) forces are usually engineered out using tubes and shafts of various kinds, with or without bearings, but always with lubricants. The linear ones are a bit trickier as they are present in every part of a moving vehicle and in static assemblies like bridges exposed to loads and the elements.

How can straight line vibrations make something move in a circle? I have a friend with a PhD in physics which came in handy for this bit! A thread is a ramp (see appendix **D: The Six Simple Machines**) wrapped around a cylinder. For a torque controlled fastener to rotate there has to be space between the internal and external threads. That means there is a tiny bit of play in every direction. When subjected to a linear force a portion of it is redirected (vectored) around that ramp. The pre-load rotate it to release tension, unless prevented from doing so.

Design Factors

Short Clamp Length : limits the amount of stretch in the shaft. That makes all the other compression factors worse because even a small amount of movement uses it up.

Paint and Coatings : applied for aesthetic and protective reasons are often easily damaged during tightening and compress or wear away over time.

Multiple Clamped Parts : no matter what they are made from, increase scope for movement or *play* in the finished assembly. This is inherent in the fact the fasteners are stiff springs. The more fasteners and layers are involved the more springs you have holding additional moving masses.

Gaskets : are essential in every moving part from a piston moving gas to a panel sealing out dust and fluids. Even thin, hard gaskets like the ones for car cylinder heads deform under pressure because that's how they form a tight seal.

External Factors

Variable Loads : are everywhere in the real world, static systems don't exist. That lovely, solid looking bridge is subject to huge variations in load as vehicles pass over it. It's exposed to wind, water and wide ranges of temperature.

Work Hardening : occurs because metals develop micro fractures which dislocate the crystal layers. Counter intuitively those dislocations stop the layers sliding past each other, making the metal harder. This process is called work hardening, which increases the brittleness we discussed earlier. The loss of elasticity in the fastener is a disaster, as it can reduce pre-load, tension and friction, weakening the assembly.

Relaxation : is another side effect of those micro-fractures. The shaft can get fractionally longer. Combine that with the loss of elasticity and you have a significant weakening of pre-load.

Compression : affects metals and plastics, even when used as a matrix for composites like carbon or Kevlar®. Particularly when subjected to the external factors like thermal cycling, vibration or both.

Thermal Cycling : accelerates and exacerbates all these processes, by expansion and contraction for metals and softening/hardening cycles for plastics.

RUSTY

The Ten Step System

If the head of the fastener is damaged, refer to the techniques in *Damaged on page 77*

This is the hub of the book for seized fasteners. The principle is to minimise risk of injury to you and of collateral damage to the items you are dismantling. The process is divided into three risk categories, increasing in aggression. The lowest risk techniques also require the fewest tools, so you can make a start immediately while additional items arrive by post.

Low Risk

Clean

Lubricate

Rock

Freeze

Medium Risk

Dissolve

Shock

Vibrate

High Risk

Heat

Heat & Quench

Destroy!

Risk Levels

Low Risk : techniques use only basic tools. They do not require heat and repetition of low levels of force. You will need a handful of consumable items for cleaning and lubrication. PPE will be mainly gloves and safety glasses.

Medium Risk : techniques need a few more hand tools, one consumable and one power tool, an *Impact Wrench see page 175.* Same PPE as for Low Risk unless the solvents state otherwise.

High Risk : techniques use special tools, extreme heat and long levers for maximum force. They make extensive use of consumables, power tools and require top level PPE for physical impact, electric shock, fire suppression and chemical protection or exposure.

Process Details

This is a suggested sequence but you can skip forwards or loop backwards. For instance, if dirty lubricant oozes out during the **Rock** step, then **Clean** and **Lubricate** again with fresh clean oil. **Rock** again.

In a hurry or need not re-use parts? You can skip straight to the **High Risk** section, or even the **Destroy** step. But be aware violence to the fastener can damage you and the surrounding components. I can hear my Dad saying "More haste, less speed," the wisdom of which took a long time and many mistakes to sink in.

Low Risk

1: Clean

Cleaning the affected fastener and bearing surfaces has several effects.

- ◆ Tools: Brushes: wire, plastic or bristle.
- ◆ Consumables: Paint Stripper
- ◆ Degreaser
- ◆ Fine Sandpaper

- ◆ PPE: Eye Protection
- ◆ Nitrile Gloves

Benefits

First, you are removing a small amount of the material causing the problem. It's still in the thread, but this is a good start.

Second, you gain visibility of the material trapped between the fastener and the assembly. The colour of this may feed into later steps involving chemicals. Reds and browns are iron oxides, greens and blues are aluminium and copper.

The third benefit is size correction. Serious contamination can give a false feeling of the size of the head under the tool. That can lead to head damage as it crumbles away, causing a slip which will damage it more. This is very helpful with internal drive heads with bevelled sides, which are prone to gouging even when clean.

The last reason to remove contamination is to help later lubrication. A crusty ring of rust and dirt will act as a barrier and a sponge, preventing penetrating oils from working their magic.

Dust/Loose Rust

Buy a set of brushes with varying degrees of stiffness, which include organic, synthetic, brass and stainless bristles. I own a set of three, the bristle part about 30mm but only 5mm wide. That means I can get into crevices. Choose the most aggressive material you can get away with without damaging the components.

Paint

You find a fastener covered in several layers of paint which may have protected the fastening. The resistance which caused you to pick up this book may be the paint itself.

Consider a judicious application of paint stripper. If you don't have a solvent, use a sharp implement to score the paint close to the fastener, then flake it off the head, breaking the seal. This also helps prevent the rotating fastener tearing off a larger area of paint. Switch to the stiffest brush possible to clean the head.

Oil/Grease

For those of us doing vehicle maintenance, this will be the most common barrier. *†Degreasers* are a well established way to disperse it. Again a stiff brush is essential even if applied with an aerosol. Rinse and dry to avoid any fires later.

2: Lubricate

At this point you can apply a *†Penetrating Lubricant* of your choice. Take the time to lubricate yourself with a hot beverage while it soaks in.

- Tools: Brushes: wire, plastic or bristle.
- Consumables: Penetrating Lube
- PPE: *Eye Protection*
- *Nitrile Gloves*

Penetrants

Once upon a time in a forum far, far away, I made the mistake of mentioning I'd attempted to use WD40® to free a seized fastener. The result was a spectacular uppercase outburst from a senior forum member who said it was the wrong tool for the job.

The †*WD-40* range has expanded to include cleaners, degreasers and a specific penetrant formula. They've even added high temperature and anti-seize lubricants too, the **Smart Reassembly** section has details on anti-seize. We've also seen a practical †*demonstration* the classic multi-purpose formula is good as a rust-buster and a water dispersant. So, if Original WD-40's all you've got... get stuck in.

They've also solved the problem of losing the straw when the elastic band perishes. The Smart Straw® shown in figure 3 Smart Straw flips down for storage and a standard cone shaped spray pattern, or up for those awkward crevices.

Figure 3 Smart Straw

The secret of penetrants is capillary action. We're familiar with surface tension from water clinging to the sides of a glass, bending at the edges. We call this the meniscus, a Greek word which translates as crescent. If you put a tube into water the circular meniscus pulls the fluid up the tube. It rises above the level of the liquid until it's weight equals the clinging force. The thinner the tube, the higher it climbs.

Water soaking up your trousers, paint moving up the bristles of a brush, oil moving up the wick of a lamp, are all examples of capillary action. We need the lubricant to flow into the space between the threads and among the cracked crystals in the rust.

Tip:

Shafts often run through unthreaded tubes which admit water and become bonded to them by rust. Even after the fastener is free, you may need to cycle through the techniques again to free the shaft from the tube. Despite the lack of thread the techniques will work, in fact they often work better. The same capillary action which lets the water in, will suck in penetrating lubricants.

While most freeing lubricants are thin in texture this is not just about viscosity. They blend penetrating oils to exhibit strong meniscus with metals and metal compounds. That's one reason I'm not a particular fan of home-brew concoctions.

One of the down sides of low viscosity is rapid evaporation. You must reapply the penetrating lubricant several times, more in warm weather. Advice on intervals vary but if you wait until the surfaces only appear damp, that covers all bases. You can do this for hours or even days before you start the job. Prep during the week for work at the weekend is a popular and wise habit.

Tip:

A great tip to reduce evaporation is to wire a ball of cotton or kapok onto the head, or the exposed part of the thread. Soak it with your preferred penetrant to prolong exposure and hold liquid in contact with the items being freed.

If dirt oozes, repeat the **Clean** step.

3: Rock

This technique applies when your first attack on a fastener frees it just a little, creating a small amount of rotation to play with. It's tempting to get a bigger lever to overcome the apparent obstruction. Please don't. We can use that tiny amount of movement to rock the fastener back and forth, cracking the crystals.

- Tools: Any **Gripper** or **Lever** which fits the head.
- Brushes
- Consumables: **Penetrating Lube**
- PPE: **Eye Protection**
- **Impact Gloves**
- **Nitrile Gloves**

Benefits

As with cleaning, this rocking motion has complementary effects.

First, if you cleaned and lubricated this works lubricant in the threads deeper into them. Each loosening movement lifts the head, letting in more lubricant. That contacts threads by the bearing surfaces, and the tightening cycle spreads it down into the hidden parts of the thread. This bears some resemblance to the way an *†Archimedes Screw* works.

Second, movement cracks the crystals, diminishing their strength, grinding them against each other to form powder. Powder is absorbent, aiding lubrication, and takes up less space, re-opening the thread gaps cemented together by the oxide compounds.

That opens up space for more penetrating oil. Repeat this rocking motion a dozen times, then spray in some lube and... drink another cuppa. Rock and lubricate are excellent candidates for repetition. Remove any oozing of contaminated lube and spray fresh lube in.

Group Effect

Here's a variation which applies to an assembly held together with many fasteners. The fastener you are working may be under load because you slackened others. Lubricate and re-tighten the surrounding fasteners to take the load off, then try the stuck one again.

A few iterations of waggle, lubricate and beverage should show increased movement. If not, use your next trip to the loo to consider escalating to the next step, freezing or a new intermediate step we call Nagging.

Nagging

The Low Risk techniques were originally designed without power tools, but I recently learnt a trick which is too good to pass up. I stole the term Nagging from my friend Rob who likes track days, and does all his own prep work. He saw it in an article praising a mid-range Milwaukee impact wrench with a maximum torque of "only" 250Nm

(184 lbf-ft) and several lower settings. The key is that it has mechanical clutch.

The trick is to start on the low settings and let the tapping of the physical clutch "nag" at the rust in the thread. As with Rocking, you are not trying to move it, at least initially, only to use the vibration to disrupt substances blocking the thread.

I was fitting a new bumper to my car and trying to transfer the fog lamps from the old one. They were attached with self tapping screws through those metal clips they slide onto plastic. Rusted solid, the first head failed even using Textured Tip screwdrivers. That's after spraying with penetrant the previous night and twice that morning.

That got me wondering. Would nagging work on a screw? I got my NoCry 1/4 inch cordless screwdriver and turned the clutch all the way down. I gave it 10 to 15 seconds at each level. That screw came out at maximum (6). But the head didn't fail. The next screw came out at level 5 and the one after that came out at level 4. The really cool part is that the NoCry has a paltry 10Nm (7.4 lbf ft) of torque and only costs £45 (about 60 bucks).

4: Freeze

Science Bit:

*That feeling when your sweat evaporates from your skin is physics in action. Heat from your body is turning a liquid to a gas by taking in energy called the †**Latent Heat of vaporisation**. The faster this happens, the greater the drop in temperature.*

The cool bit (sorry!) is you can speed up the process by using a clever cocktail of chemicals. You use volatile compounds which prefer to be gas at room temperature and pressure, then you compress them into an aerosol can. When you release them, they disperse into gas, cooling the item you sprayed.

You can lower an item well below room temperature, 21 Celsius, 69.8 Fahrenheit. My preferred product claims it can lower an item to -43 Celsius, -45.4 Fahrenheit, though I suspect the phrase "in ideal conditions" is in the fine print somewhere. It's a tiny change compared to the increase from a heat source, but it works because the lubes only need a tiny space.

- Tools: Any *Gripper* or *Lever* which fits the head.
- Brushes
- Consumables: *Freeze Spray*
- PPE: *Eye Protection*
- *Impact Gloves*
- *Nitrile Gloves*

Benefits

Several mechanisms are in play here, which is why it's so effective.

The Fastener : hole will enlarge by freezing. Cold metal contracts, but that doesn't make the hole smaller, it makes the ring of the fastener thinner. That enlarges the hole and shortens it, which also lets lube into the bearing faces.

The Shaft : portions exposed to the spray will cool and shrink, opening a small gap between the threads and the fastener. This is the primary reason you have to wait 30-60 seconds after the spray before applying force, to let the coldness propagate.

The Head : on a shaft also shrinks, letting lube into the bearing surfaces.

The Rust : won't contract as much as the metals when cooled. The crystalline oxides can't follow the large, rapid movement. It's like a delicate glass cylinder trapped between the two threads.

The Thread : is now much more exposed to the penetrating lubricant all these products contain than with standard room temperature lubricant. It's listed in a separate step as it's volatile and more hazardous. If used in a confined space, I'd wear sealed eye protection and a mask intended to protect you from vapour, not particulates.

Low Risk Loop

The Low Risk steps are all excellent candidates for repetition. That's how I got the brake calliper off the car. Time now saves tears later.

Medium Risk

5: Dissolve

Why is this solution not in the section under Cleaning? Two reasons: The first is that *some* solvents are hazardous. We'll cover this in the next section. The second, less alarming, reason is that this step takes time and might be fiddly. Low Risk may ask you to make a drink while things soak in, but solvents need time to work, up to 24 hours.

What this does have is a very high chance of success. The solvent can expose surfaces that the previous steps couldn't get to.

- Tools: Brushes recommended for solvent.
- Consumables: Rust Solvent
- PPE: *Eye Protection*
- *Nitrile Gloves*

Risks

Some, not all, are potent, corrosive chemicals, very hazardous if you get any in your eyes. Some are not safe in contact with your skin or if inhaled, and some are carcinogenic with regular exposure.

Second, they are messy. You need to paint, pour or spray them onto the areas you are treating and there will be drips, overflow or over-spray.

Third, you need to know what you're treating. I was looking on the net a few days ago and thought I'd found the perfect one. Then I noticed it said, "Not suitable for aluminium." Avoid a nasty surprise, always read the label.

What are the parts made from? Some of the most stubborn bolts on a car are suspension components. These often contain bushes made from rubber, silicone or polyurethane, which may react with some of these fluids.

Solvents

It's important to thoroughly dry the area, removing all residues from the Low Risk steps. This is to to give the solvent unobstructed access and to ensure we don't accidentally create a toxic combination.

Science Bit:

White vinegar, $C_2H_4O_2$, in a kettle dissolving calcium carbonate, $CaCO_3$, uses the same principle. A chemical reaction turns it into gaseous carbon dioxide, CO_2, and a soluble solid, calcium acetate, $Ca(C_2H_3O_2)_2$ dissolved into water, also produced by the reaction.

Let's get this out of the way. You *can* remove rust with vinegar the same way you can trim your toenails by amputating your foot. For clean steel the vinegar is reacting with the metal first, creating rust and then the rust to create ferric acetate. If it's already rusty it will dissolve the rust into water soluble ferric acetate first, then attack any exposed metal to create more rust. One guy left some rusty tools in a bucket of vinegar for 18 months, turning a ring spanner into a pry bar and a 0.75" spanner into a 0.8" spanner.

The ideal product will dissolve rust and electrolytic corrosion products, but be inert with the underlying metal, see **†Rust Solvents**. I use an exceptionally safe product called **†EVAPO-RUST®** which I saw on the **†Project Farm YouTube channel**. It contains no acids or alkalis, is non-toxic and biodegradable. Dissolves all oxides of steel and iron, while having no effect on:
- Copper
- Brass
- Aluminium
- Plastics
- Vinyl

You can rinse your items or hands using only water and there are no special conditions for disposal, other than iron held in solution.

The only downsides are, it needs to be above 18℃(65℉), and best results come from leaving the item for at least 24 hours. The need for warmth will be a problem on outside jobs in the cooler parts of the year.

If the item is part of an assembly, you need a way to keep the liquid solvent in contact. The †*EVAPO-RUST*® container suggests soaking high quality paper towels held in place with magnets.

If you really want to immerse it like you would a detached part, you need to make a temporary bath. If the surface is horizontal, make a ring of †*Sugru* or other mouldable glue around it, if it's vertical fashion a cup shape, like an uplighter. Don't use an epoxy putty... you'll struggle to get it off! This technique may cause damage to some types of surface. If in doubt, use the paper towel method.

Low Risk Loop 2
Once drained and dried off, repeat all the Low Risk steps. The solvent should have dissolved rust, opening gaps and exposing surfaces. That will massively multiply the effect of the first 4 steps.

6: Shock
Time for a sharp shock to the pesky oxide crystals. It might help to hit it with a BFH (big f****ing hammer). It is better to focus the force at places, and in directions of our choosing.
- ◆ Tools: *Manual Impact Driver*

- *Cold Chisel*
- *Brass Drift*
- *Steel Punch*
- *Hammer*
- Consumables: *Penetrating Lube*
- *Freeze Spray*
- PPE: *Eye Protection*
- *Impact Gloves*
- *Nitrile Gloves*

BFH

This is counter intuitive. Use the biggest, heaviest hammer you can deploy in the space. It's easier to aim a slow mass than a small mass moving faster.

Science Bit:

$$KE = \tfrac{1}{2}\, mv^2$$

Kinetic Energy (in Joules) = Half the Mass (in Kg) x Velocity (metres per second) Squared

You can see, for the same speed of movement, more weight is more energy. Small increases in velocity have a big effect because we square velocity. If the first few swings don't work you only need to tap harder, not swing like a psycho.

An Impact Driver : is the best tool for this if you own one, and smart first special tool purchase if you don't. What we need is to send shock into the tube of crystals while also applying torque, this fat handled screwdriver does that. Inside it has a short shaft with a ramp which rotates when you hit the top. They come with a square drive for sockets and an adaptor for chunky, hardened screwdriver bits to engage internal drive heads.

Use hardened sockets, colour coded black. Even if you own an Impact Wrench (from which you can borrow the sockets) try the impact driver first as a lower risk, more compact option with higher shock force down the shaft axis.

Hand Tools

If you don't own an impact driver, you can produce some effects using a punch, drift or chisel to focus the shock. The smaller the tip the better, as it multiplies the pressure per square inch at the point of impact.

Science Bit:

Pressure per unit area works for solids and fluids (gases and liquids). A person weighing 135 lbs sits on a 5lb stool with a 1 inch square pad on the floor, the pad will exert a pressure of 140 PSI, 140 lbs on that square inch. We can multiply or divide that pressure. If we enlarge the pad to 2 inches per side, the area is 4 times and the pressure per square inch is 1/4... only 35 PSI. If we halve the pad to 1/2 an inch, the area is a 1/4, which multiplies the pressure by 4... 560 PSI! Now you can see why stiletto heels leave marks on a wooden floor.

The Bearing Surfaces : There may be a bond between bearing surfaces of the fastener and head. We need to direct some focussed force into that zone. Place a chisel or punch at 45 degrees in the junction of head and surface in the centre of the face. If possible, go around all six sides giving them a few good whacks. Lubricate, make a brew… Repeat this cycle two or three more times (without the tea) then try Rocking again.

You can send shocks down through the shaft using a drift or punch in the centre of the head. Punch is least likely to slip, a drift is better if you need to preserve the fastener for re-use.

You can use hand tools as a poor, risky, substitute for the twisting action of an impact driver. Place the chisel blade at 45 degrees near the corners instead of the centre of the face, and tap the head in a lefty-loosey direction. Wear gloves and don't hammer towards anything which will scratch or bleed if you slip!

7: Vibrate

Just to be clear, the Impact *Driver* described in the previous section is a manual tool for applying both torque and longitudinal shock. An Impact *Wrench* is an electric or pneumatic power tool, applying and releasing huge torque force only.

This is the grown-up version of the Nagging technique we discussed earlier. If you own a mid-range impact wrench and one of the monsters, start with the mid-range, set it low and work up to the maximum, then switch to the BFW.

- Tools: ***Electric Impact Driver***
- Pneumatic Impact Driver
- Hardened Sockets
- Consumables: ***Penetrating Lube***
- ***Freeze Spray***
- PPE: ***Eye Protection***
- ***Impact Gloves***
- ***Nitrile Gloves***

Good news, if you invest, this is the point where you often win the fight. Garages make quick work of jobs we sweat over for days is because of these powerful tools. If you don't need one long term, consider renting...

Science Bit:

Great force over a short distance is the key. If you're wondering why your wrists don't break, the answer is gearing. Imagine holding an engine in first gear, where many rotations with low force reduce into fewer revolutions with higher torque at the wheels. The gentle oscillation you feel is an even smaller movement at the business end, but with tremendous force.

High Risk

8: Heat

I've talked to several mechanics during research for this book. Other than the pneumatic impact wrench, they use this technique most. But if there's collateral damage they have public liability cover, full fire gear and trained first aiders. Plus, they aren't picking up the bill... you are.

◆ Tools: Any *Gripper* or *Lever* which fits the head.

- *External Heat*
- Consumables: Paper Towel to dry off lubes.
- PPE *Fire Extinguisher*
- *Fire Blanket*
- Fire Resistant Gloves

Heat works best when applied to a fastener on a shaft rather than a shaft screwed into a threaded hole in an assembly.

Science Bit:

At school in the late 70s they used nothing more complex than a perspex tank full of polystyrene balls on a device with a platform. At first they were all just lying in the bottom, there were visible gaps between them. Then my physics teacher turned on the device. It vibrated, adding some energy to the system.

The balls bounced around, bumping each other. This widened the spaces between them so the total volume in the container increased, the surface was riding higher. As the power climbed this process continued. It took no imagination to realise enough energy would bounce some out of the container, like melting a solid or turning liquid to gas.

Risks

There's some risk of damage to the fastener and surrounding areas. If the temperature difference between the exposed shaft and the area under the fastener is too great, it causes a stress fracture.

Also beware the heat will transfer into the spanner... that's why you must wear heatproof gloves. There's a possibility of damaging the spanner. Tools use complex heating and cooling sequences to harden them. Sudden uncontrolled heating and cooling may undo all that. Keep the duration of contact as short as possible.

You may set fire to stuff... including, but not limited to, you! However, we've placed this in Medium Risk because we can mitigate the risks with the correct safety equipment.

Some of you will already have searched auction sites for used oxyacetylene gear. But even second-hand they are expensive to buy and run, also difficult to use without training. You also need to be careful because of the hoses to the torch nozzle. If damaged, they can leak and... terrible things happen. This level of expense and aggression, fun as it is, isn't necessary.

The melting point of steel is around 1,370 °C or 2,500 °F, depending on the carbon content. All the gases bar butane can melt your fastener to a molten blob. You may even end up with a droopy shaft. No one wants that.

The idea is NOT to try melting the oxides seizing the thread. Their melting point is between 1,377 °C for Iron(II) oxide and 1,566 °C for Iron(III) oxide. You will melt or wound your fastener, your shaft and the surroundings before they reach melting point.

Some types of anti-vibration lock nuts use a plastic insert in the top. We will destroy this and the fastener will be toast, requiring replacement.

Prep

Always clean the area around and behind the place you will apply heat. That removes flammable debris, or liquids already present, plus those applied earlier.

Avoid using heating techniques near:
- wiring
- pipework
- rubber
- plastic
- paintwork

I use a 1m x 1m fire blanket to help shield delicate components in the vicinity from heat damage. Domestic plumbers use these as they have no choice about operating blow lamps near flammable materials.

The phrase most used to describe how hot you should make an object is "dull red" or "cherry red". We're talking real cherries here, not those silly bright red things they put in drinks in the 70s... ahem, or so I'm told. This is difficult to see in daylight, that's why a blacksmith's forge is so dark inside. Consider setting up some shade to ensure you don't overheat things.

Mechanisms

WARNING: Safety

WEAR GLOVES.

WEAR EYE PROTECTION.

USE A FIRE BLANKET.

HAVE FIRE SUPPRESSION TO HAND.

REMOVE ALL LUBES AND FLAMMABLE MATERIALS.

TAKE CARE WITH PARTS WHICH MAY BE WEAKENED.

As with most of these processes, several factors are at play. First, while heat won't melt the brittle oxide compounds, it works like the opposite of the freeze spray. It will stress them as the metals expand and contract.

Second, the fastener is a circle. As the circumference expands the diameter gets bigger. This releases the pressure on the trapped oxides. That's why you aim to undo the fastener while still hot.

The shaft gets bigger too, but aim to heat the fastener the most. It will absorb heat through conduction despite the trapped oxides acting as an insulator so it won't expand as much as the fastener.

The Candle Trick Doesn't Work

This is a popular internet tip for wheel nuts and easily accessible fasteners away from flammable areas. You hold an unlit candle on its side above the wheel nut or bolt. Heat the fastener, letting the heat wash melt the wax from the side of the candle, dripping onto the nut at the bearing surfaces.

Older versions of this book include it as something to try but I can now tell you not to bother. My hero Todd Osgood at *†Project Farm YouTube channel* has tried it in his usually thorough fashion, while testing a group of known penetrants. He then cut the nuts off with an angle grinder and you can clearly see the penetrants work, the wax does nothing.

9: Heat & Quench

The theory here is identical to the Heating section except we're using shock cooling. This places even further stress on the compounds causing the problem.

- ◆ Tools: Any *Gripper* or *Lever* which fits the head.
- ◆ *External Heat*
- ◆ Iced Water
- ◆ Consumables: Paper Towel to dry off lubes.
- ◆ PPE *Fire Extinguisher*
- ◆ *Fire Blanket*
- ◆ Fire Resistant Gloves

<u>WARNING: Safety</u>

WEAR GLOVES.

WEAR EYE PROTECTION.

USE A FIRE BLANKET.

HAVE FIRE SUPPRESSION TO HAND.

REMOVE ALL LUBES AND FLAMMABLE MATERIALS

Iced water speeds up the cooling phase, the shock cooling having a more severe effect on the delicate oxides. This may expose an existing weakness and the shaft will fail. At least it's off and at this step, that's progress. There are ways of extracting the stump.

<u>WARNING: NOT Freeze Spray</u>

Under no circumstances use any of the freeze sprays for the quench step. They often contain

flammable compounds. Use good old fashioned water, with ice if you can get it.

10: Destroy

At this point in the book, I owe you an apology. I expected the previous techniques to solve your problem. The following sections are brief because there's not much to say. The techniques are simple, brutal and should be effective. If the shaft has snapped, skip to *Snapped* for ideas on extraction.

- ◆ Tools: *Nut Splitter*
- ◆ *Angle Grinder*
- ◆ Consumables: None
- ◆ PPE: *Eye Protection*
- ◆ *Impact Gloves*

Let's Split, Scoob

This only applies to a nut on a shaft, not a bolt in a tapped hole. You need specialist tool called a Nut Splitter, they come in sets with each one covering a range of nut sizes. I've listed it in the high risk section because we are dealing with significant levels of rust. Even if the nut splits with relative ease, we're likely to damage the underlying threads.

<u>WARNING: Eyes</u>

Wear eye protection.

Stop sniggering at the back. This is serious. For a bolt in a tapped hole you can ignore this step. *Nut Splitters* split the fastener away from the shaft. We're in the section called Destroy, don't expect the thread on the shaft to emerge unscathed from this process.

Grinding

Grinding Off : works for a nut on a shaft or a ruined bolt head where the techniques in **Head Damage** failed. It almost guarantees thread damage, as you won't be able to tell if you cut into the nut until afterwards.

Disassembly : is a special case. An assembly where the shaft passes through something into a threaded hole. For multiple fastenings, consider taking the whole thing apart by grinding off all of them.

The downside of this radical approach is that you have multiple headless shafts to remove, the upside is that the attached assembly is out of the way, granting access. Apply the lubricating and freezing techniques to get lubricants into the threaded hole. The section **Snapped** has ideas on extraction.

WARNING: Eyes/Ears/Hands
Wear eye, ear and thick hand protection.

Grinding a Slot : can apply to fasteners or shafts. Applied to fasteners it works in much the same way as the **Nut Splitter**. Use a grinder or oscillating saw to cut a slot in each side of the fastener. Whether hex or square cut into opposite faces. Power tools mean this won't work in a confined space. Choose two opposing faces with enough access for a hammer and chisel, or at least **Spring Loaded Punch**.

If you're careful not to slice all the way to the thread, you can re-use the shaft. Unless it's a rare piece of old equipment, you can't get parts for, replacement is safer. One or two sharp blows into each of the slots should finish the job or you can just grind all the way in. If you are replacing the entire fastening, cut right the way to the threads.

DAMAGED

If the damage is to the thread skip to *Thread Damage on page 92*

If the damage is a sheared shaft there's a dedicated section for that *Snapped on page 99*

There are several ways a head can become damaged. We're assuming you have cleaned the fastener up to remove all rust or corrosion products.

Environmental Damage : is the most obvious. Stainless steel is too hard in some applications, titanium and plating is more expensive. Steel is the most common and rust will affect any in contact with water, road salt and mud.

External : drive heads are seldom so damaged that they shrink but they can change shape. Hex fasteners are weakest at the corners. Weakening, weathering and rounding caused by previous work, increase the risk of a slip using a standard spanner.

Internal : drive heads suffer more because dirt and water sit in the drive hole. For the same shaft diameter the internal drive will always be smaller in diameter than the external one, magnifying the proportional damage. It may change size and shape, losing the ribs and flutes which engage with the tool.

Physical Damage : is the other reason heads can be hard to remove with standard tools. It may result from poor design in the assembly inflicting wear and tear on the head. More, likely use of the wrong tool, wrong size of tool, or a force not perpendicular to the head. When a tool slips the fastener is often damaged. Repeated, unsuccessful attempts make that worse.

Head Damage

Externally Driven

DON'T PANIC! says the Hitchhiker's Guide to the Galaxy in large friendly letters. It is important that you apply or re-apply one or more the techniques in *Low Risk of Damage* section first. Otherwise you'll wipe off another pair of corners or do more damage.

If the damage is severe it creates two problems. First the item is no longer the same size, it is smaller corner to corner. Second the metal is jutting out as a burr which changes its shape, and can foul the tools intended for it.

Quick and Dirty

Let's start with some quick and dirty solutions not requiring special tools. You should use these as a last resort, if you're too skint to buy tools or in a big hurry. Please, read the rest of this section first.

Two More Bites

If you damaged all six shoulders of a hex head in one go... remind me to never upset you, then skip to **New Faces on page 81**

- ◆ Tools: Crescent spanner or standard socket.
- ◆ Brushes
- ◆ Consumables: **Penetrating Lube**
- ◆ PPE: **Eye Protection**
- ◆ **Impact Gloves**
- ◆ **Nitrile Gloves**

Verify the spanner is the correct size and engages with no free movement. The jaws should touch the complete face, not a point near the shoulders. If rust or damage has made it an odd size, or if it's not quite the right size of spanner, try an **Adjustable Spanner.** Or, switch to the **Wall Drive** spanners mentioned later in this section.

A standard jaw, open ended spanner will usually only round off two of the six corners of the head, you have two more chances. Move the spanner 120° to one of the two remaining pairs of faces. Better still switch to a ring spanner or socket driving all six if they will slide on past the damaged bits.

New Faces
- ◆ Tools: ***Adjustable spanner.***
- ◆ Brushes
- ◆ Consumables: ***Penetrating Lube***
- ◆ PPE: ***Eye Protection***
- ◆ ***Impact Gloves***
- ◆ ***Nitrile Gloves***

Another simple approach is to file or grind the damage off the faces. Remove the smeared metal creating fresh, undamaged flats and sharp corners. Check for play with a ring spanner in the original size. If there's a lot of play you'll need an adjustable or wall drive spanner.

Spanners in different size standards might fit the new size you created. Metric and imperial sizes are often different by tiny fractions, ideal for a smaller fastener. Grind off a minimal amount and try the next smaller spanner size. If one close match is too small and the next one up is too big, keep filing until it's a snug fit.

Special Tool Solutions
These tool based methods are all faster, safer and less risky than the quick and dirty solutions. In these days of ultra-fast delivery 7 days a week the best tool may be only 24 hours from being in your hand.

Multi-Pin Socket
The next best solution is a specialist tool I call a ***Multi-Pin Socket*** but search for "gator grip." It's a 3/8th hex socket stuffed with a matrix of hexagonal pins, each with a spring underneath. These pins displace to

accommodate almost any shape which fits inside the cylinder. There are great product videos showing it undoing damaged hex nuts, square nuts and even wing nuts. Hex nuts with burrs are trivial for this beast.

Wall Drive

The ring end of a **Wall Drive** spanner is the best option if available, or you can leave the job long enough to buy a set.

These are only available for hex shaped external drive heads. Instead of a shape which matches the head, they use curved lobes to drive the walls, the flat faces, away from the weak corners. This has two beneficial side effects.

Each spanner can fit heads from several different size standards including metric, imperial and US systems. This reduces the number of spanners in your toolbox. The lobes touch the faces at different points for each size.

Of more interest to us, the lobes avoid the damaged shoulders and burrs, in fact the spaces between the lobes give the burrs additional space. That means they may fit straight on without messing around grinding the damage off.

Figure 4 Metrinch Ring End
†*Metrinch Spanners*

†*Metrinch Sockets*

Mole Grips (Locking Pliers)

If it's a mashed mess *Mole Grips* are the last heat-free method. Developed in 1955 by Thomas Coughtrie (1917-2008) while managing director of M K Mole and Son. The first locking pliers having been the brainchild of William S. Petersen in 1924.

Figure 5 †Neji-saurus Jaw

These **†Neji-saurus® pliers** have a simple, but effective modification to the jaws to aid in gripping a head from above. The v-shaped cuts in the jaws lock onto the corners of external drive heads. On a screw (neji in Japanese) they dig notches into the circular head.

If you've never used them before its a simple process:
1. Clamp the jaws into the locked position.
2. Twist the adjuster screw so the jaw is slightly wider than the head.
3. Place the jaws over and twist the adjuster so they touch it.
4. Press the unlocking lever.
5. Twist the adjuster tighter by about a quarter turn.
6. Clamp so there's a kind of over-centre feeling and it locks.
7. If you don't feel it, repeat 4-6 until you do.
Twist the fastener or hold it while you spanner the other end.

Weld on a Lever
Use a welder to attach a steel rod to the top of the damaged head, at 90 degrees to the shaft. For bolts you can attach the rod at one end to make an L-shape or the centre to create a T-shape. When cooled you

use the lever to unscrew the fastener. The heating and cooling cycle also aids loosening.

Alden Grabit Pro

   The †Alden Grabit® Pro will work perfectly on bolt heads up to about M6 (size 14). Use a centre punch to create a dimple for the drilling phase and proceed as you would for a gouged out screw. Full procedure in the section Reversible Drill/Taps for damaged screw heads. Don't attack the blister pack with side cutters (like I did) the instructions are inside. In case you just bought it without jumping forwards: BOTH DRILL AND TAP USE THE DRILL IN REVERSE.

Internally Driven

Internal drive fasteners are common on prestige cars. They often get damaged because people buy cheap tools. The tool bit fails, applying force to the fastener cavity at the wrong angle. That causes collateral damage removing material and depositing material too.

Camming Out

Drive openings fall into two categories: vertical or slanted.

The slanted sides are an intentional design feature causing the tool to "cam-out" of the head. This prevented fasteners shearing off in the days before torque control existed. In practice this now causes more problems than it solves.

Vertical Sides

Even heads with vertical sides can cam out if the fastener is weather or worn, or the bit is sub-standard. It can also happen if the operator cannot exert enough pressure down the axis of the shaft or if access issues force the tool away from the vertical.

Slippery Slopes

With either design, a head damaged will deteriorate. The damage lessens the amount of force needed for a second and subsequent cam-outs. Each repetition makes things worse.

Tip:

If you've had a cam-out: STOP! Follow the steps below...

If the bit and fastener both took damage, discard the bit for an undamaged one. It was news to me that these are consumables, but the fact many bit sets, even of high quality, come with duplicates confirms that is the case.

Textured Tips

There are several companies like **†Wera®** making enhanced bits and tool tips. Some have abrasive diamond coatings, others tiny grooves or ribs to dig into the sides of the opening. These inhibit the cam-out effect. If you don't use these they are helpful as future prevention and as a solution to the current damage problem.

Figure 6 †Wera Lasertips

The diamond dust coating on these increases frictional engagement with bevelled heads.

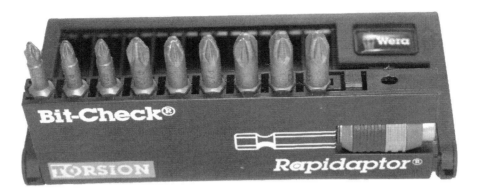

Figure 7 Wera Diamond Bits

True Grit

Great things start to happen when you do deep research into a topic. One of those things is that sales platforms notice what you are looking at and make helpful suggestions. Some of those are things you didn't even know existed. *†Screw Grab* is one of those things. It's a gel you apply to the screw head to enhance the grip of standard bits.

If you already have coarse *†grinding paste* it is viable alternative, a small pot in two or more textures is a good buy.

Bushfix

A bushfix solution is to stretch a rubber band across the screw head and press the bit into the rubber. This can mask imperfections and improve purchase.

Impact Driver

If you use these techniques but get a second cam out switch to an *Impact Driver* or even an *Impact Wrench*.

Reversible Drill/Taps

As this is a destructive method I've left it later in this sequence. However, previous steps have no effect on how well this works - which is extremely well.

Alden (I assume it's the crescent ratchet people) have a product called the †Grabit® Pro. Double-ended combination drill/taps which go as low as Size 6 screws up to Size 14, equivalent to an M6.5 bolt. BOTH DRILL AND TAP USE THE DRILL IN REVERSE.

Figure 8 Alden Grabit Pro

You use the drill end IN REVERSE to drill out the original slot/cross hole. The drill end has a shoulder to stop you going too deep, shearing there head off the shaft.

Then flip them the bit over in the chuck to use the matched tap to lock in the perfectly sized hole IN REVERSE. I just removed two countersunk bolts I couldn't reach because the walls of my sockets were too thick using these. I had tried before using inferior knock-offs which didn't work. This is confirmed on Project Farm where Todd tested a set of each and the Alden Grabit® were far superior.

Epoxy Putty Spanner

This is going to sound ridiculous, but I've tried it and it worked. One of the key fobs for Sue's car wouldn't open because the slot in the battery cover was damaged. The plastic lid was designed with a slot for a large coin, but someone had used a smaller coin or a screwdriver. Doing this repeatedly wore the vertical sides into ramps.

The plastic was quite soft, the root of the design flaw, but the tattered, roughened plastic was also a good keying texture for something sticky. I don't remember exactly what I used, but it was a two part epoxy putty similar to *†J-B Weld Steelstik* - a top performer in Todd Osgood's tests on *†Project Farm YouTube channel*.

I thoroughly cleaned and degreased the battery cover, mixed the putty and moulded it on. Because it was an internal drive slot I took special care to press the centre firmly into the slot, carefully keeping the putty confined to the cover. Finally I moulded it into a flat shape with sloping sides.

Leaving it for a couple of days to be absolutely sure, I picked it up and twisted it... Success! It turned to the unlocked position and came out, to be replaced by a new one.

Will it work with smaller fasteners and external drive heads? Hard to predict. Save this trick for situations where other ideas can't be used or have already failed.

X Marks the Slot

For single slot screws use a micro-grinder or small file to restore the vertical sides. This can also work for crosshead and geometric shaped holes where all the drive ribs have gouged, just create a simple slot. Use *Cleaning*, *Lubrication* or *Freezing* before any renewed attempts. Clean away any residue before using the friction enhancers suggested earlier for another attempt.

Thread Damage

A stripped or crushed external thread is a qualified win for us during extraction. With the shaft removed we can, disassemble the parts for examination and repair on the bench. We always replace a damaged shaft if possible. If it is not, because of scarcity or lack of availability, the steps below may allow reuse.

WARNING: Reuse of Damaged Shafts

Reuse no fastener components used in a safety critical application like car brakes or major supporting elements.

REMINDER: Threadlock

REMINDER: These processes are best done with cutting lube. For thread lock the bore and shaft will need prepping. Use a Degreaser, make sure they are clean and dry.

Stripped External

Damage during tightening means you've either tightened into a fouled thread or stripped it. You can't, and shouldn't, try to bully the fastener past the damaged section. For minor damage can be fixed in the next section. If the threads are stripped you must discard because you have probably exceeded the elastic limit.

For assemblies don't forget the remnants of the stripped fastener inside the internal thread. Clean as described in the section on *Stripped Internal* threads.

Damaged External

Sometimes an external thread gets crushed or gouged. There are two solutions to this.

The first is to use a *Die* to remove the burr and restore the thread with some sections missing but still usable. Only appropriate for larger bolts used in groups, but never in a safety critical application.

Alternatively, you can trim thread damage near the tip of the thread provided it is still long enough and you have a complete helix of thread. The best tool is a bolt cropper, because the jaws bite in parallel to the threads. Make sure the two jaws are in the same thread channel. A hacksaw will work but you must cut at the thread angle and perpendicular to the shaft. Either way, you must check for burrs and partial threads and file them off.

Stripped Internal

A stripped internal thread in a nut is unusual, the external thread on the shaft is usually the casualty. As we told you, bolts come in a wide variety of metal alloys with unique characteristics for hardness and elasticity to suit the application. The only requirement for a nut is to be harder than the bolt. A stripped fastener is trivial as we can replace it, where the bottom component has the thread machined in, that may be difficult or expensive to replace. A cheap component is best replaced. This next section needs specialised equipment, a high level of skill and plenty of time. If you must reuse... here goes!

The internal thread will contain remnants of the shaft thread, clean by running a Tap of the same size and pitch down the bore of the hole. A 12.9 Class bolt in the correct diameter and pitch is a good backup if you don't yet own a tap and die set. You should grind at least two vertical slots into the thread of your improvised tap to collect the detritus you are cleaning, clamp it in a vice and wear full protective gear: eyes, ears and gloves. Fill these slots with *cutting lube* to aid the process and pick up the muck you are dislodging.

Wind your tap in and out until it turns with finger effort only. Resistance means serious thread damage which may cause weakness when reassembled, reconsider replacement. Don't forget to degrease, and dry the hole, in particular if you intend to use thread lock fluid.

Thread Replacement

<u>WARNING: Eyes</u>

Wear protection for your eyes and ears. Hand protection also advisable, swarf under your skin is nasty.

Failure in the previous step means the thread is damaged beyond repair and must be remanufactured to avoid weakening the final assembly. You can buy thread repair kits in exact diameters and thread pitches.

A major player in this field has become synonymous with this technology, but trademark lawyers get twitchy about that stuff. The kit should include the tap, several hardened coils and an insertion tool. Some even include a T-handle or an adapter for your square drive ratchet to turn the tap and later to install the coil. The kits come with detailed instructions, please follow them. I'll describe the process here so you know what you're getting into.

The drilling out is very similar to the previous section. You are aiming to remove the damaged thread, to leave a smooth hole. Use the drill size specified, or provided in the kit. Clear all swarf from the hole using your preferred method. Please be careful!

Tip:

For those of you who don't do lots of metal drilling, I made a mistake you can learn from. I was struggling to drill out some captive nuts but my bits were past their best. Becoming impatient, I got out my old electric drill, turned it up as fast as it would go and tried again. Big mistake. It got hot, smoke started coming off it, but I made little progress. I had a rest and tried a couple more times. The tiny shavings got less with each attempt, then stopped.

Frustrated I headed indoors and did a bit of mulling and talking to people on Facebook. It slowly dawned on me what I'd done. I'd work hardened the metal I was trying to drill. Exactly as I described in How things Loosen, the heat cycles had hardened the metal I was drilling. I had become frustrated, ignored my own advice and failed to apply my knowledge and common sense.

There are several things I should have done to avoid this:
- Stop and buy sharper bits.
- Use a slower speed.
- Use a Cutting Lube.
- Press a bit harder.

The solution was a set of *†M42 Cobalt drill bits*, made from a molybdenum series steel alloy with 8 percent cobalt. I switched back to my trusty cordless drill driver, in first gear, not second. Then I dripped on some *†Molyslip MWF* (Metal Working Fluid) and the metal shavings were back - minus the smoke!

The next step is to reduce our oversized hole back to the original size with the hardened coil, which has threads inside and out. Tap the enlarged hole to the outside thread, then screw the coil into the hole with the insertion tool.

Tip:

Ensure the hole is free of contamination using compressed air. Take great care to protect your eyes and ensure no one else is in the vicinity. Ensure the hole is dry, unless advised otherwise.

The last step is to fit the hardened coil which reduces the thread to its original diameter and pitch. Again the kit should include a tool or adapter for turning the coil. The coil has a tail across the bottom, otherwise the insertion tool would go all the way through. Screw the coil onto the insertion tool, then screw the coil into the hole, stopping just below the surface of the original piece.

<u>WARNING: Eyes</u>

Wear protection for your eyes and ears. Hand protection also advisable, swarf under your skin is nasty.

Unscrew the insertion tool leaving the coil in the hole, the insertion tail may snap off of its own accord or you may need to use a flat tipped punch. It will always drop into the hole! Extract the broken tail by tipping it out for small assemblies. For heavier stuff, use a magnet. If you use compressed air in some form, mind your eyes!

Intentionally Blank

SNAPPED

All the heating, chilling, hammering, levering and dissolving, even arranged in order of aggression, can cause an occasional casualty. You get movement but you can feel something isn't right. You get a large sudden movement, causing grazed knuckles, or a strange shearing like hard cheese. Now you're staring at a sheared stump. It may protrude, or be flush with the surface, so these techniques are in two sections.

Protruding Shaft

There are more options for extracting a protruding shaft than one which snapped off flush to a surface.

Stud Extraction

For home DIY people these are not wooden battens under plasterboard. Stud in this context is a threaded shaft with no head at either end. They use studs a lot in cars, for instance in the hubs to attach the wheels using nuts.

Stud extractors are the perfect tool for extracting the projecting stub of a sheared bolt, which is almost identical to a purpose made stud. Each tool has pros and cons. See the **Stud Extractors** in the **Special Tools** section.

Time For T

This technique involves drilling a hole across the shaft to insert a cross piece. We can only use this technique with a long stump and large diameter fasteners. For two reasons:

- ◆ You need enough shaft left to take a decent load.
- ◆ You need a thick crosspiece or it will just bend.

The force you can exert will be less than you can bring to bear with a spanner. Extensive *Cleaning*, *Lubrication* or *Freezing* before this is mandatory. The alternative is to attach a T-piece or Lever using a welder as described under *New Head*.

Flatten & Twist

For thick shafts (10mm or more) you have the meat to create new flats to apply force onto. You can grind flats onto either side of the shaft and use *Locking Pliers* or a *Adjustable Spanner*. But you can spread the load by grinding the shaft square using a square drive spanner. This puts load onto four corners instead of only two and gives you the best chance of recovering.

Tip:

Some self assembly furniture uses square nuts. They slide into slots as captive fasteners. This means the kits include small spanners with three sided square openings, worth keeping hold of a few after assembly.

New Slot

This is the same trick as we used to repair a gouged out slot in the section on *Head Damage.* You can turn the sheared shaft into a slot or cross headed shaft. Use a *Hacksaw* or *Grinder* to create a slot or two slots at right angles.

New Head

The first technique, Lock Nuts, is the quickest, least expensive and least damaging. The remaining techniques all need an arc welder. If you are in this part of the book, things are serious, you may need to get one to solve your problem.

Lock Nuts

This only works for a stump with space for two additional nuts. For large fasteners you can cut a nut in half at 90 degrees to the shaft, making two slimmer lock nuts, the texture from the cut will even help them lock together.

Screw the first (bottom) nut on leaving room for the second (top) nut. Screw the top nut on finger tight until it has the stump flush with its top surface. Hold this nut still with your fingers and *unscrew* the bottom nut it until it reaches the top one. Hold the top nut still with a socket, set to tighten, using a spanner to **unscrew** the bottom nut against the top one as hard as you can. This should jam both nuts so they don't move. Remove the socket and use the bottom nut for all anticlockwise operations and the top one for all clockwise ones.

Use A Nut as a New Head

Welder owners, screw a single nut onto the snapped off shaft and weld to the top of the stump. This is tricky if the stump is short as you're welding inside a hole.

Avoid heating the stump too much, causing a stress fracture which snaps the stump off flush. The cause is big temperature differences between the exposed shaft and the hidden part which is a huge heatsink. Keep welding bursts brief and allow plenty of cooling time between tack welds.

One possibility to avoid this overheating is to use epoxy resin to attach the nut to the snapped shaft. Screw it on and drizzle the resin into the hole in the nut, taking care the epoxy doesn't seep through the thread, making matters worse. You must clean up to use heat afterwards.

Construct One

Arc welding can build a new "head" of fresh material from the filler rod. You can make this new outcrop any shape you want, but keep things simple by making something flat to grip with *Mole Grips* or other pliers.

Re-Attach It

You can try to reattach the snapped head to the shaft. The neatest way is an autogenous weld, metal to metal with no filler. The current from the welder fuses the head back onto the shaft. Works best on smaller shafts. Failing that you can tack weld it onto the stump with a hard filler. The heat generated in the shaft from this activity often helps loosen the offending shaft... once cooled off!

T-Piece or Lever

Another option is to attach a rod to the item you're trying to remove, that gives more leverage than the original head.

The shock heating in all these techniques disrupts the materials seizing the shaft. With an arc this heat is more localised than with an external heat source like a blow lamp.

Flush Shaft

Your options are more limited here. Buy or borrow tools designed for this specific situation.

Reverse Tap

Reverse Taps are the easiest and least risky solution. They work like a **Reverse Thread Socket**, but you're screwing a left handed external thread into a hole.

First you drill a pilot hole which is smaller than the shaft and larger than the tip of the reverse tap. This pilot hole should go the entire length of the shaft if possible. The vibration and twisting force of the drilling can help disturb the rust holding the shaft in place. Material removed down the centre makes space which releases pressure from the thread.

Engage the reverse tap and turn lefty-loosey. The reversed thread bites into the pilot hole and the tapered tip tightens down winding the shaft out.

Attach a Nut

You can *Use a Nut as a New Head* for a shaft snapped flush. Clamp an undersized nut to the surface over the stump and weld inside the hole.

Cut It Out

Drill small holes around the perimeter of the stump until it comes free. Use a larger fastener in the resulting large ragged hole. You can also drill it to remove the raggedness.

Drill Out

<u>WARNING: Eyes/Ears</u>

Eyes and ears. Hand protection also advisable as swarf is nasty under your skin.

Sometimes the thread is in something we want to re-use. The aim here is to clear the shaft from the existing thread without damage. If re-use isn't critical or there's no thread, you can be less precise. This takes the correct equipment, sound technique and time. But done well it's one of the best solutions once the problem has escalated this far.

You need to find your centre. Take a deep breath and relax. Getting this step wrong can ruin this technique, so take your time. Done from first principles, the geometry looks like this.

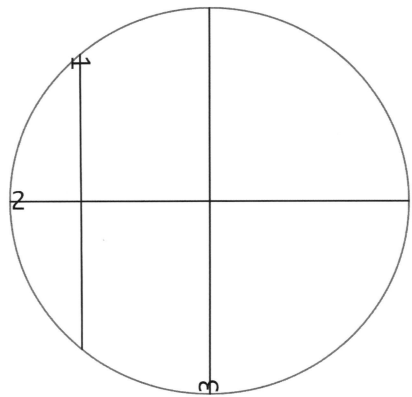

Figure 9 Finding Any Centre

Chord 1 Make a chord across the circumference, measure and divide by two, marking the half way point.

Chord 2 At 90 degrees to chord 1 going through its marked half way point. Measure that, halve and mark the halfway point.

Chord 3 You can either use the mark on chord 2 as your centre or score a third chord at 90 to it, making it easier to see.

Figure 10 Centre Finder

By far the easiest way is to spend the price of a pint on one of these centre finders. Put the stump into the junction of the L-shape and draw or score a line, turn it approximately 90 degrees and draw another. The point where those two lines cross is the centre. This is trickier to do if the shaft has broken off flush or recessed. If you buy a see through one you can use the edges of the hole.

Use a centre punch to dent the centre to keep the first bit centred. Drill the pilot hole to less than half the diameter of the shaft, then progressively enlarge using bigger bits.

A threaded shaft has two diameters. One is overall diameter of the thread, one is the central solid part of the shaft after we cut the thread into it. What you are aiming for is to match the diameter of that solid core leaving a helix of disembodied threads. When the centre is perfect, you remove the drill bit to find the threads peeling away from the inside of the hole. If you're off centre there will be a crescent on one side and partially exposed threads on the other. Pull out the big bits with needle nosed pliers, airline the rest, with eye protection.

If there are remnants use a tap to clear them from the hole. You need to know the exact diameter and pitch of the shaft you sheared to ensure this works.

Hot Boring

I picked this up from a TV program where they were dismantling large pieces of heavy industrial equipment. An excellent alternative for large bolts is to melt out the centre of the shaft with a gas torch. We can't give you a minimum size because it depends how small and well confined the flame is but M12 or M14 upwards seems reasonable.

The combines aggressive expansion and the void in the centre, which lets the shaft relax away from the bore wall. Hot and brief should work best and prevent too much heat soaking into surrounding structures, weakening them.

Punch Out

Another trick for shaft stumps in unthreaded assemblies is to punch them down the axis. Will work well with Hot Boring, but remember to let the other parts cool to avoid them welding to or annealing your punch.

Big Hammer

A big punch with a lump hammer, or even a sledgehammer wielded by a trusted assistant should do the trick.

Power Chisel

If the brute force approach doesn't work repeated vibration using a power chisel or air hammer with a round bit fitted is the way to go.

Build a Bypass

This applies most to screws, as heads fail part way out. You can cut off the protruding screw remnants with a Hacksaw or Bolt Cropper or even a decent pair of Side Cutters. Cut as close as possible to the surface. Put a new screw parallel to the old one, far enough away to avoid splitting the material. A pilot hole is a good idea but don't drill too close to the original.

Intentionally Blank

SMART REASSEMBLY

We have used patience and restraint to free the fastener, preserving the parts in our assembly. It will benefit us to prevent the problem recurring in the future.

Friction .vs. Tension Review

Our approach will depend on the joint. If it uses ***friction enhancers***, cleanliness and sealing out moisture without lubrication are key. A ***tension joint*** locked with wedge-lock *†washers* or a castellated nut could use lubrication to smooth torque and exclude moisture.

An assembly meant to be held together by friction enhancers like thread-lock or nylon enhanced fasteners must be cleaned, failing to do so could be disastrous.

Tip:

*Reassemble wedge-lock washers with care, the ramps should be interlocked in the middle and the radial grooves on the outside faces. Remember, through bolted assemblies need two washers, one for the nut and one for the bolt head. If unsure, use these links to access the manufacturer's website: **†Nord-Lock® or †Heico-Lock®** which include torque guidelines.*

Cleaning

You can clean rust from the thread by applying grinding paste to a shaft of the same diameter. Wind in and out a few times. You should see the red colour in the paste. Flush out with degreaser and use paper towels wound into a probe at each corner to dry it, taking care to get to the bottom of blind holes. Keep cleaning until they come out clean and dry.

Lubricants

These substances can do one or more of these functions:

- Anti-seize to prevent †*galling* (tearing off chunks).
- Physical anti-rust and anti-corrosion shielding.
- Chemical prevention of galvanic corrosion.
- Lubrication for improved torque setting accuracy.
- May set to inhibit loosening.

Torque & Clamping Force

Here's a strange fact about lubricants. The engineering industry, unless otherwise stated, gives torque values based on a dry thread. A torque wrench will show that torque as a reading or an audible/tactile click at the preset value. As discussed in **How Fasteners Work**, applied torque correlates with the clamping force. That applies to all bolted joints.

This has caused confusion on the internet, with people stating lubrication can cause you to accidentally apply too much **torque, stripping threads**. That's wrong, because the torque wrench will still show the same reading or click at the preset value. The confusion arises because people confuse the torque force perpendicular to the shaft, with the clamping force along the shaft.

Lubrication *will* increase clamping force in the tightened fastener because lubrication decreases friction in the thread. That means the shaft turns further before the opposing friction rises to the value set on the torque wrench. A bit of research shows recommendations to reduce the torque on a lubricated fastener by up to 20 percent to keep the clamping force the same. In some assemblies this doesn't matter. But sometimes it does.

Spark plugs, for instance, have a complex set of shaped washers which allow it to stay sealed during expansion and contraction. Those washers demand a very exact space to work. Many brands avoid getting into torque. They tell you to screw the plug by hand until it contacts the cylinder head, then add a specific fraction of a turn with a lever. If they specify a torque and you lubricate the thread, you'll increase the clamping force on those washers, damaging them. You may even strip the threads in aluminium heads without hardened thread inserts.

That's a direct clash with the advice for wedge-lock washers. They use lubrication and ***increased*** torque to stretch the bolt shaft. We can't foresee every circumstance, these simple rules should avoid most problems. Unless specified, DON'T lubricate:

- ◆ Assemblies with pressure sensitive washers.
- ◆ Mixed hardness assemblies.
- ◆ If in any doubt about loosening.

Selection

Here's a small choice with different properties which products use as ingredients. Any overlap is because some do one job only, others do one well with useful side effects.

Fastening Replacement

Ideally, you discard a fastener as a matter of course if you go beyond the Low Risk zone. Change them if you see visible damage, or it's used in a safety critical joint.

Fastener Specs

Rummaging through your biscuit tin of old fasteners is fine as long as you take care. Do not replace them based only on length, diameter and thread pitch. They rate bolts for hardness and the percentage they stretch before they fail. You must adhere to the exact specification in documentation.

†ASTM International Standard

Anti-Seize Compounds

Anti-seize is lubrication designed to prevent adjacent surfaces binding, or cold welding, which occurs because of high clamping force, large dynamic or static loads and coarse surface textures.

They come in the form of a grease laced with a release agent. Copper is the best known release agent, with the products often called copper slip. Aluminium is a common alternative to copper. For high temperatures they use molybdenum and other hard elements and compounds. PTFE and other dry lubricants ground into powder are also popular. These all either melt, fill microscopic surface textures, act as tiny bearings or some combination of those.

Grease is used chiefly to move the powders into the thread. They aim many at high temperature applications, where oil or grease evaporate or degrade. Some products specify two maximum temperatures, for the grease and the release agent.

Aluminium Grease

The lesser-known twin of the copper grease in the next section, applied where you can't use copper with other materials in the assembly.

Approx Temp :

> **Min: Any sub-zero**
> **Max: 800-1100°C (1472-2012°F)**

Copper Grease (aka Copper Slip or Copper Ease)

Copper anti-seize looks like the solid metal, great for high temperatures, but other metals and rubber can be an issue.

Approx Temp :

> **Min: -40°C (-40°F)**
> **Max: 1150°C (2100°F)**

Nickel Grease

Used with stainless steel and nickel alloys, and available in food safe versions. Use as an alternative to other compounds. Has one of the highest temperature limits we've seen.

Approx Temp :

Min: -55°C (-67°F)

Max: 1450°C (2642°F)

Anti-Galvanic

For friction based fastenings we can use a jointing compound which excludes moisture, insoluble even in marine engines, boat rigging and other saltwater environments.

Duralac® sets hard. I applied this to a hose coupling, then had to delay the job, and it set. When we continued it was very difficult to clean out of the threads. That brittleness when set is useful when stripping for maintenance. When you see jointing compounds, or revisit one you sealed, the Rock and Freeze steps should work. If they don't, Vibration will.

Duralac Yellow (aka Canary Shit)

Approx Temp :

> **Min: Not found.**
> **Max: Not found.**

Original yellow formula uses barium chromate to block electrolysis. When the metals are the same, it inhibits rust and corrosion, when they differ it blocks conduction. We do not recommend using this to protect your food from the lasagne cell effect... the taste is awful! To avoid doubt, that was British humour...

A friend of mine works in a boatyard, he's found this in many assemblies and threads, even metal to wood surfaces to inhibit moisture ingress. Once cracked, protected joints do come undone with greater ease than those without protection.

Duralac Green

Green in colour and purpose, this is a chromate free more environment friendly version of the yellow stuff which works even better than the original.

Approx Temp :

> **Min: Not found.**
>
> **Max: Not found.**

Thread Locks

This is similar to the jointing compound above, but designed only for threaded fasteners. They are a liquid plastic which acts as a lubricant on application, setting to a pliable semi-solid.

The primary selling point of thread-locks is to prevent vibrational loosening, but sealing thread space and coating it helps exclude moisture. Not all electrolytes are liquid, but most use water as a solvent, so blocking it means no electrolysis. There is a †*wide range of products* from large load and high temperature, to ones which are easier to remove.

Threadlocker: High Temperature

Used for high heat, high force and shock load parts, like engine valve trains and gearbox components.

Approx Temp :

```
Min: -55°C (-67°F)
Max: 200°C (392°F)
```

Thread-Locker: Easy Removal

Use for fasteners under 6mm where there is a risk of shearing with stronger formulas.

Approx Temp :

> **Min: Not available.**
>
> **Max: Not available.**

Thread-lock: High Tensile

Very high strength thread locker which may take over 24 hours to set, check directions for minimum and maximum thread size.

Approx Temp :

> **Min: -53°C (-65°F)**
>
> **Max: 150°C (300°F)**

Thread Lubricants

These are simple lubricants used to ensure the fastener tightens without torque spikes. Some limited anti-seize properties in the short term, that is not their primary purpose.

Threadlock

Warning: Please take care to understand the assembly so you use the correct method for reassembly. You should check a workshop manual, not copy what you found on disassembly. If in doubt, ask. Someone may have switched the joint from friction to tension, or the opposite.

Lithium Grease

Lithium makes the grease thicker and less likely to run, or drip. This makes any application work longer and helps prevent unsightly and dangerous contamination of nearby items.

Approx Temp :

Min: -18°C (-0.4°F)
Max: 145°C (293°F)

PTFE Sprays

Science Bit:

†Polytetrafluoroethylene (PTFE) *is the most interesting substance here. A long, heavy chain-shaped molecule discovered by Roy Plunkett at DuPont in 1938, while attempting to create a new refrigerant.*

Contains only two elements, carbon and fluorine (C_2F_4), is inert (non-reactive), hydrophobic and has one of the lowest friction coefficients of any known substance. Famous as a non-stick coating for cookware, now used in dozens of applications to reduce friction and improve cleanliness. Dark grey on cookware it's a white waxy substance in grease.

Spray versions often evaporate, leaving a dry coating of powdered PTFE on the surface to work in with use. Very popular in dust exposed applications, like bicycle chains, because it can't adhere.

Slick 50® Spray

My first exposure to this was a cream coloured grease by Slick 50®, which also produces engine and gearbox additives for vehicles. The latter is the subject of many heated internet debates, but we're not going there!

Direct metal-on-metal contact with no ongoing lubrication is where this stuff seems to excel. I've noticed the protection is long lasting; a friend and I lubed the ramp on a sticky latch as a test and it lasted several years. Unavailable last time I looked, there is a dry *†aerosol version*.

Approx Temp :

Min: Not found
Max: Not found

Ultra Tef-Gel (aka Tefgel)

†Ultra Tef-Gel® originated in aerospace and has found a second home in marine rigging. It has lubricant, anti-seize and anti-galvanic properties.

Approx Temp :

Min: Not found
Max: Not found

Silicone Grease/Spray

Water repellant, non-melting grease for creating airtight and waterproof seals in pipework. Can protect porous coated metals against salt water spray damage. Should be safe with most plastics.

Approx Temp :

Min: -50°C (-58°F)
Max: +280°C (536°F)

Molybdenum Disulphide

†Molybdenum Disulphide suitable for bearings under high load or shock loads and in dusty areas. The temperature range is narrower restricting applications.

Approx Temp :

> **Min: -20°C (-4°F)**
> **Max: 140°C (284°F)**

Intentionally Blank

APPENDICES

A: The Right Tools for the Job

Bare Essentials

It's likely you own most of these items, the rest you should invest in before you start to avoid delays. If you don't want to buy the more expensive ones, then rent or borrow them.

If you see *†* visit *†TheRustyNutBible.com/links* to see them online.

Trivia:

Borrowing tools is one of those areas that seems to activate the primitive part of the brain. Manipulating objects in our environment as tools was a significant factor in our evolution. That means we have a deep attachment to tools, particularly hand tools. Please treat tools you borrow, and those from whom you borrow them, with respect. If a breakage occurs, own up promptly and apologise. Buy a replacement in consultation with the lender. Please don't ask someone who uses their tools to make a living to lend them to you, unless you are in the same trade. Eye-watering, red faced laughter can often cause offence when aimed at you.

Grippers

Pliers come in many shapes and sizes for grasping heads with different damage patterns. You can change your attack to angles which are not possible with rigid spanners or sockets.

Trivia:

This is a straight lift from the French word plier, pronounced plee-yay, meaning to bend.

†Grippers

Combination Pliers

To most of us, these are just pliers. Their full name is combination pliers, because the jaw has three separate areas. There's a flat serrated part at the front, then an elliptical opening in the centre with coarser serrations. Just ahead of the pivot point, for most *Mechanical Advantage*, there should be a pair of cutters.

Figure 11 Combination Plier

The rounded opening is useful for grasping round section shafts, the coarse serrations can grip damaged fasteners. Use the flat section for square heads or shafts filed or ground to flat sides. When intending to use any pliers with a fixed pivot, create a shallow bevel because the jaws don't shut parallel.

†Combination Pliers

This narrow non-locking version of the *†Neji-saurus* jaws is great for dealing with heads which are flush to a surface like wood or plaster. Pictured with a large wall plug we extracted from a plastered wall in our lounge.

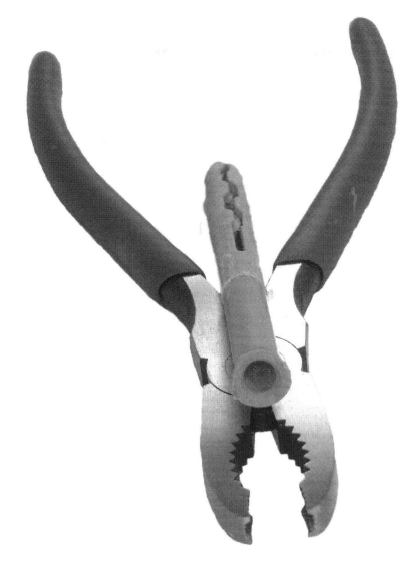

Figure 12 †Neji-saurus Narrow Jaw

Locking Pliers

Like pliers, these are handy when dealing with odd shapes. Separating clamping and twisting means your finger muscles don't have to hold the jaws shut while your arm muscles pull. That exerts more force in both operations.

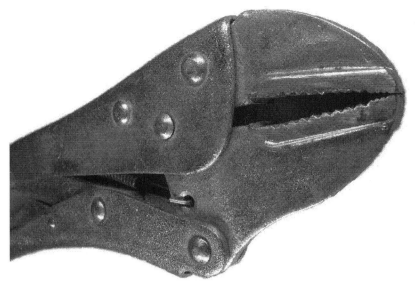

Figure 13 Locking Pliers Standard Jaw

There are many sizes, jaw shapes and jaw angles. The threaded adjuster lets you change the gap of the jaws and the over-centre point where they lock. The spring loaded tab releases the jaws again.

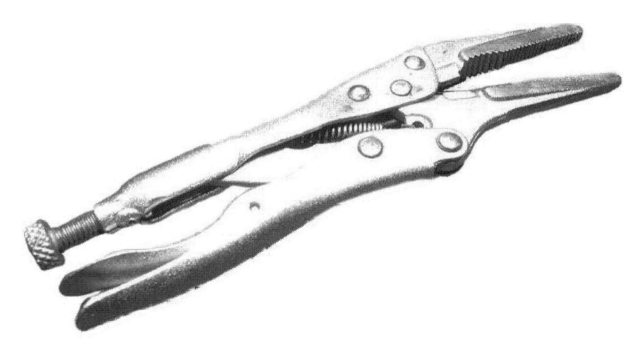

Figure 14 Locking Pliers Long Jaw
†Locking Pliers

Slip Joint or Waterpump Pliers

These are great for large objects because we can set the jaws wide. Key features are the long handles for improved grip force and the adjustable pivot point used to widen the jaws.

Figure 15 Pipe Wrench Alligator Jaw

Designed for large diameter nuts and collars found in plumbing. A big fastener means a longer thread with more contact area, creating more friction, so the handles are longer to overcome that.

You should gap the jaws so they are as close as possible to parallel when clamped on to maximise the surface area of the serrated jaws. It also avoids damaging the corners of the object.

Figure 16 Pipe Wrench Widened Jaw

There are handle lengths from 10 to 16 inches (250-400mm) with various jaw shapes. The ones shown here are alligator jaws for obvious reasons. There are also hooked raptor jaws and ones with a semi-circular void. The jaws are slimmer than standard ones because plumbing sometimes uses thin hexagonal nuts. This may be useful in a confined assembly.

†Water Pump Pliers

Clamps

Spring loaded clamps are of little use here, but any which close using a screw mechanism are. Also a cheaper alternative to multiple pairs of Locking Pliers if you need to grip a lot of things at once or one thing in many places.

†Clamps

Vice

This isn't for the job. It is very useful for detached assemblies. Also for extracting items removed with a **Reverse Thread Socket** or **Reverse Tap**. I removed some locking wheel nuts I'd lost the key for with reverse thread sockets. Backing them out required clamping the nuts into a large vice and using the same 600mm breaker bar I'd used to remove them.

†Vice

Levers

Levers are one of the oldest mechanical tools, there's a detailed discussion of *The Six Simple Machines in an appendix*.

†Basic Levers

Crow Bars

Named for the v-shaped crow's foot at the most curved end, there's a similar shape without the notch, at the other end which has a shallow bend.

We do not use these to manipulate fasteners, but to move things or hold them still. Use either end, jamming an assembly against a nearby solid object. For a shaft rusted in a hole or tube, try holding the fastener still and apply force to the assembly.

Figure 17 Crow Bar Foot

Use the tail end as a wedge to hold an assembly which moves, so the force can transfer to the shaft.

Figure 18 Crow Bar Tail

†Crow Bars

Torque Wrench

An interesting way to kill two birds with one large lever is to buy a torque wrench. The ones which go up to 3 digit numbers have nice long handles, plus you can tighten wedge lock washers to the correct value. That said, a **Breaker Bar** is cheaper, see **Big Guns**.

Figure 19 Torque and Standard Ratchet

†Torque Wrenches

Spanners

There are three features for a spanner:

- ◆ Length
- ◆ Thickness
- ◆ Jaw shape

Variants include semi-circular spanners and ones with offset jaws. We do not cover those here, but the same basic characteristics apply.

†Spanners

Spanners vary in length, becoming longer as the size increases, because larger fasteners tighten to higher torque and need more effort to move. It is also a simple way to reduce the possibility of shearing smaller fasteners.

If you are short of tool storage space, and if you already own a socket set, consider a **Breaker Bar**. Most applications only use a subset of sizes you can find listed somewhere on the web.

In a nutshell, slimmer is better for restricted areas where a thicker jaw won't fit. Make sure you buy a reputable brand because you need high quality steel alloy jaws, chrome-molybdenum (CrMo or Chromoly) is common.

Standard Spanners
Aerospace tools will fit exotic fasteners with amazing precision in a heat controlled environment. The jaw will spread force along at least two opposing walls of the head. But a worn or rusty fastener, after cleaning, may be smaller. If the weather is cold, metal contracts, so some tools design slack in. The effect is they may place load on two opposing shoulders of a hex head rather than two opposing faces.

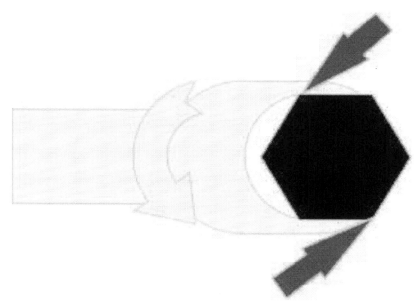

Figure 20 Hex Shoulder Stress Points

The back part of some spanners is hexagonal, rather than rounded, increasing the number of points of contact from two shoulders to three, but still inferior to other options.

Ring spanners are best with six out of six, remember "Ring is King." As a bare minimum, try to use a *Flare Spanner*, designed to tighten the collars on pipes like the brake lines on cars. The name springs from tightening the collar over the flared end of the metal pipe. There's a narrow gap just wide enough for the pipe to pass through and bear on five out of six faces.

Adjustable Spanner
This is one of the most useful things to keep in your toolbox to bridge gaps in your fixed spanner set. Also useful if you own a full set in one standard like Metric, but sometimes work on fasteners in another.

Figure 21 Adjustable Spanner

Also a neat solution to contraction in cold weather and for worn away fasteners. Also useful if you ground away damage on a fastener to a size which may not match *a* fixed spanner.

This new design of self-adjusting spanner has all the advantages of the older design but is simpler to use. The angled handle pointing away from the rotation means the circular jaw constricts when you pull it. The harder you pull, the tighter it closes, you flip it for loosening or tightening.

Figure 22 Self-adjusting Spanner
†*Adjustable Spanners*

Metrinch Wall Drive Spanners
Some designs of jaw and socket solve the problem by driving the head via the walls of the fastener. The crescent end of this design has lobes, driving four faces rather than two corners.

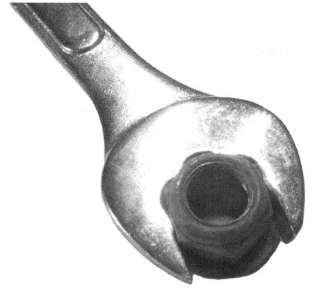

Figure 23 Four Point Wall Drive

The bumps contact the hex head away from the fragile corners. Voids between the bumps means we can use it on a hex head with damaged shoulders, you don't even need to grind off the damage.

Ring spanners are still best, driving all six walls of the head.

Figure 24 Six Point Wall Drive

A second effect is they fit multiple sizes. The bumps come into contact with the wall a different distance from the corner. This blurs the boundaries between Metric, AF, BA, Whitworth and BSF size standards. This example fits 19mm, 4AF, 3/8w, and 7/16BS. Incredible.

†Metrinch

Wera Joker Spanners

These are innovative tools for several reasons. The open ends need only 30 degrees of movement and has a serrated plate on one side serving two purposes. Uppermost it stops the jaw dropping off the head onto the shaft.

Figure 25 Wera Joker Up

When lowermost, grips the head to prevent rounding the shoulders.

Figure 26 Wera Joker Down

The ring ratchet is an unusual 80 tooth design needing only 4.5 degrees to trigger it.

Figure 27 Wera Joker Ratchet

†*Wera Joker*__

Flare Spanners

Flare spanners are a ring spanner with a gap through which a pipe or threaded bar can pass. Made to tighten compression collars on pipes, they can also run a nut along a threaded bar.

Figure 28 Flare Spanner

Tip:

Sometimes a head or shaft close to another surface will not admit a ring spanner. But the gap in a flare spanner may allow it to fit through.

You can even buy **_††Ratchet Flare_** spanners, bet you're wondering how they work... I know I am, why not have a look?

†Flare

Sockets

As with spanners, sockets have three features:

- ◆ Depth
- ◆ Drive
- ◆ Shape

Sockets come as a matched set with basic drive handles in standardised drive sizes. You can also buy extra ratchet handles with additional features and buy sockets to extend your range and to replace lost or damaged ones.

This gives you a great deal of flexibility to expand your system for specific problems. If you have a head at an awkward angle, buy a gimbaled ratchet handle. An extra large nut on a vehicle fan or wheel, buy just that size.

Sockets are deep, a characteristic spanners lack. For a hex shaped head in a hole, like a spark plug set down into a cylinder head, a spanner won't work, but a deep socket will. They are also available shortened to fit into tight spaces.

The vast majority of sockets are square drive and one of the last bastions of the old imperial system of measurement. Square drives are available in 1/4", 3/8",1/2", 3/4" sizes. For our purposes, these are the core sizes. Trucks, quarry machinery and oil rigs use bigger. The bigger the drive is, the longer the handle. There are also unconventional drive solutions like the Vortex system described below.

Not all socket sizes are available on all drives. A big drive with a long handle would shear a small fastener and a short handle is next to useless on a large fastener. But even within a set there is overlap to give you options when space is tight.

As with the Ring Spanner there is almost zero chance of damaging a head with these, you are driving all six corners or walls.

The Wikipedia page is interesting... *†screw drive types*. The shape you will most encounter is still the hexagon. There are a surprising number of ways to grip that simple shape.

†Sockets

†Socket Handles

†Socket Sets

Six Point Sockets
    The dominant shape is a hexagon which works 99% of the time. We're dealing with the 1%. The head is rusty and may have damaged shoulders from a previous removal attempt, both problems distort the head shape.

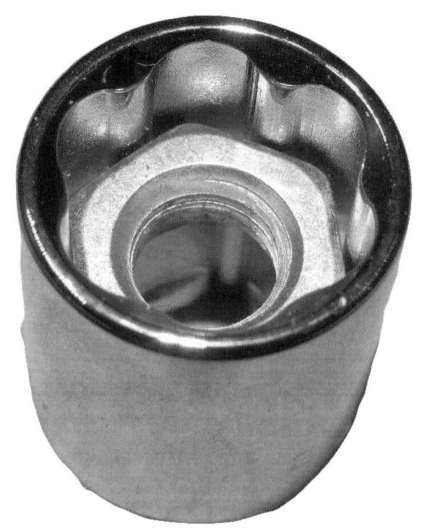

Figure 29 Six Point Sockets

The solution to both problems is the same, use sockets which drive the sides of the hexagon.

†Six Point

Pass Through

Pass through systems drive outside the socket, engaging at six points rather than the four of the square drive. That makes it strong... not that I've ever sheared a square drive, but you can dream, right?

Figure 30 Vortex Socket

Better still, the centre is hollow, so it can accommodate lengthy protruding shafts or threaded bar, which passes through the centre. How cool is that?

†Pass Through

Metrinch Sockets
I've owned a set of Metrinch® Spanners for over ten years now, and they're excellent.

†Metrinch

Draper Multi-Drive
The primary purpose of these is for use with bi-hex heads, two hexagons overlaid with one twisted 30 degrees, but you can use them for hex heads.

Figure 31 Draper® Multi-Drive

If you weren't aware twelve point bi-hex heads existed, join the club! Neither was I until I did the research for this book!

†Multi-Drive Sockets

†Multi-Drive Sets

Multi-Pin Sockets
These are standard hex shaped sockets packed with spring loaded pins. I've seen hexagonal and square pin designs.

Figure 32 Multi-Pin Socket

This design adapts to the shape of any damaged fastener, no matter how many corners burr over. Provided the shape isn't almost round this little gizmo should get a grip. It can even turn:

- ◆ hooks
- ◆ eyes
- ◆ wing nuts
- ◆ square nuts

†Multi-Pin Sockets

Impact Sockets

They make impact sockets from chrome vanadium steel alloy, hardening them to withstand high torque and continuous exposure to large shock forces. They use a black phosphate finish by convention. Beware of imitations, buy a known name from a reputable source.

Figure 33 Impact Socket

These, by Draper®, have a rounded void at each corner. This means they'll fit okay onto heads with damaged corners and engage the side wall away from those damaged areas. Nice touch.

‗†Impact Sockets

Hammers

It's better to seek forgiveness than to ask permission, and better to swing a big hammer slowly than a small hammer quickly. The philosophy of this book is to defer extreme violence, but focused shock is an integral part of the low risk methods we'll use early.

‗†Hammers

Lump/Club Hammers

You can use a standard hammer, see below. I'm told the thing about exploding hammer heads is an urban myth. However, a fragment may detach from the object you hit. We've included impact tools aimed at improving accuracy, reducing the risk to you and damage to the surrounding parts.

Figure 34 Lump/Club Hammers

†Lump Hammers

†Club Hammers

Slide Hammers

Used for pulling motions to remove dents, these are more accurate and less likely to crush your fingers. The changeable tips include hook shaped ones you could apply to a head where there is no room for a conventional hammer. I'll admit haven't tried this yet, it's here as something to try if you have one.

†Slide Hammers

Mallets

Non-damaging hammer is like saying non-lethal weapon. After deaths happened they stopped calling them that, now it's "less lethal," which is odd because you can't be less dead. So, less damaging and less likely to dislodge a fragment. You should wear eye protection, anyway.

Also less likely to dislodge the offending head or the tool being struck. Don't hit the thing you are trying to remove, use a punch or chisel which aims to concentrate the force into a focused chosen place and direction.

Figure 35 Multi Mallet

†Mallets

Dead Blow Mallets

Reduced-rebound mallets look standard but contain an internal damping mechanism. to decrease bounce back. When striking steel, which has more elasticity these are worth considering. A friend made one using plumbing supplies and lead shot, making a T-shape and filling the cross-piece.

†Dead Blow Mallets

Brass & Copper Mallets

These mallets reduce rebound, sparks and damage to the struck tool.

†Brass Mallets

Impact Focus

In the heat of the moment it seems tempting to hit the fastener with a hammer. Take a deep breath and use tools to focus force where it will do most good...

†Focus Impact

Brass Drifts

Brass punches, or drifts, are not the first choice for the techniques described here. We can transfer most force using steel punches. Use these softer tools if you need to avoid sparks, damage or fragments. They are semi-sacrificial items designed to deform in preference to the struck item.

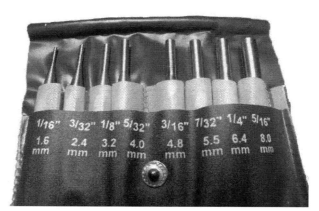
Figure 36 Brass Drift

These tools will mushroom and burr in use, but you can grind or file them, shortening until they need replacing. Probably not in your lifetime!

†Brass Drifts

Cold Chisels

The chisel shape means you can place the edge in the ninety-degree angle formed by the head and the surface. The aim here is to disrupt any rust products visible at the surface without shearing the head from the shaft.

Figure 37 Cold Chisels
†Cold Chisels

Steel Punches

Don't scrimp on these, buy a reputable brand. You are hitting a piece of hardened steel into another piece of hardened steel, a shard can always fly off of the fastener. You don't want to add the possibility of a piece coming away from the punch by purchasing a cheap knock-off.

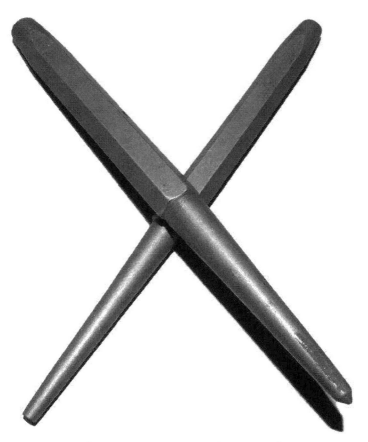

Figure 38 Steel Punch

†Steel Punches

Spring Loaded Punches

These are good for creating a dimple in a precise position to engage a manual punch or to stop a drill tip slipping. They don't have the same energy a steel punch hit with a BFH, but you can compensate for this by using more strikes.

Figure 39 Spring Loaded Punch
†Spring Punches

Manual Impact Drivers

You may think this is a heavy handed thing to put under *Bare Essentials.* As discussed earlier, the brittleness of the materials seizing the fastener is their weakness. The potent combination of shock and torque makes these tools an absolute must. And they don't cost a fortune.

Figure 40 Manual Impact Driver

All kits come standard with a set of hardened screwdriver bits. Good kits come with a 1/2" adaptor for use with hardened **Impact Sockets**.

Hitting it translates some downward energy to a rotational force, the rest fires down the axis, shocking the brittle compounds seizing the thread. On a screw head, the downward force minimises the possibility of camming out. See **Cam Out** for details.

†Impact Screwdrivers

Saws

These are cheap and versatile. No toolbox should be without one. Their compact size and short stroke make them ideal for confined spaces.

Mini Hacksaws

Framed hacksaws were the only game in town. The frame gets in the way, but these compact blades have nothing.

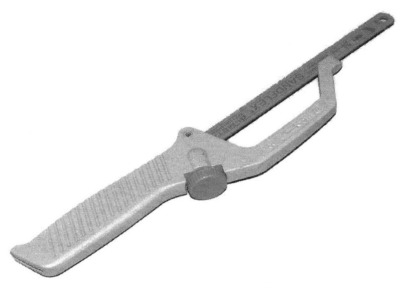

Figure 41 <u>Mini Hacksaws</u>

Junior Hacksaws

These are brilliant for confined spaces. Get a pack of blades at the same time. They come in three shapes: straight, L-shaped and arched.

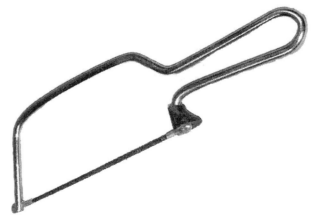

Figure 42 Junior Hacksaws

†Junior Hacksaws

159

Frame Hacksaws

These aren't usable in confined spaces but have a much longer stoke if there's room.

Figure 43 Frame Hacksaws

†Frame Hacksaws

Cable Saws

These tools come up as camping equipment or as emergency saws for survival kits, but can sever a seized shaft in a confined space. The key advantage is you get a longer stroke than you can with a reciprocating saw.

†Cable Saws

Consumables

Here are a few things it pays to have a stock of to save you from having to pop out in the middle of the job.

Saw Blades

There is no point scrimping on quality, you'll only end up with shrapnel injuries. There doesn't seem to be any standard nomenclature for these. Manufacturers have their own attachment mechanisms and codes. Blades fall into wood/plastic, ceramic and metal for both reciprocating and oscillating tools. Coatings are like the ones in the *Drill Bits* section.

Drill Bits

Drills are simple but sometimes misunderstood. Drills don't use friction, they use cutting. We don't sand a potato; we peel it. The hardened tool steel shaft has a sharpened tip. They get hot, but only when misused. Helical grooves along the shaft remove waste from the bored hole, like water from an Archimedes screw.

The primary characteristic a drill bit requires to function is hardness. Providing the bit is harder than the material being drilled, it will cut into it and keep its edge. The bigger that difference, the longer it keeps an edge before you have to sharpen or discard it.

There's a downside. You knew there had to be a catch, right? We talked about brittleness in the introduction, about rust. Hard metals can also be brittle; vulnerable to sudden force or to force applied to a small area.

Throwing a stone at a standard glass window is a sudden point of force which will shatter it. They use glass in reinforced plastic to protect it from shock and point impacts; the strength is because it bonds to the resin matrix and doesn't stretch.

This means the very hardest materials can snap if we apply sideways forces, they are better suited to use in bench drills and other machine tools. You might get away with it if you use a **Drill Guide**.

The harder materials have one significant benefit, they withstand high temperatures better.

You should always lubricate the bit with a proper cutting lubricant. It might still get hot, in which case you should stop and allow it to cool.

Never exert high pressures on a drill bit. Press it, don't lean on it. Let the torque and the cutting edges do the work. As long as material is emerging, it's working. A new HSS (High Speed Steel) bit is cheap, but having to stop mid-job to drive out and get one is a pain.

†Drill Bit Selection

Bit Materials

Uncoated Bits
The solid bits are right at the centre of the hardness/brittleness conflict. We list them in order of ascending hardness. You need to take care to exert force down the centre of the bit for the hardest ones.

Another advantage is, you can sharpen rather than discard them. There are various drill sharpeners available. Some are standalone units with their own motor, others use the drill itself as the power unit for the sharpener.

†Drill Sharpeners

WARNING: Low Carbon
For wood only, DO NOT use these to drill metal.

High Carbon Bits

We can use these for wood or metal, but they lose their temper if they overheat so High Speed Steel (HSS) bits have replaced them.

High Speed Steel (HSS) Bits

This is where things get serious. These bits are hard and should be suitable for our purposes here. They withstand heat better than High Carbon, so we can run them at higher speeds, use a lubricant anyway.

†High Speed Steel (HSS) Drill Bits

Tungsten Carbide Bits

Solid carbide bits are for industrial applications where they need many hours of use without having to halt an assembly line to replace it. Expensive and brittle, but okay in machines which control the angle and pressure.

You can get bits where only the cutting tip is tungsten, the rest of the shaft made from something cheaper and less brittle. The best of both worlds! They hold an edge well and drill pretty much anything, hard metals and even masonry but not tungsten carbide.

†Tungsten Carbide Drill Bits

Cobalt Bits

These are harder than HSS bits and can drill stainless steel and other hard materials. They are very resistant to high temperatures but more brittle than HSS, keep only downward pressure on the bit.

†Cobalt Drill Bits

Boron Bits

A specialised bit for removing spot welds in Boron steel, commonly used in cars to save weight.

†Boron Drill Bits

Coatings

Don't dismiss these as poor substitutes here. We're not talking about a light spray of gold paint, unless you buy poorly. These coatings extend the life of the bit between three and five times over HSS bits.

The underlying base bit in most cases is HSS, so these aren't brittle like the hardest of the uncoated bits. This makes them more suitable for hand tools.

Black Oxide Coated Bits

The cheapest of the bit coatings, but easy to fake, when genuine it provides a slight increase in longevity and corrosion resistance. We recommend you spend more for one of the Titanium variants described next if you can.

Titanium Nitride (TiN)

This is a ceramic coating for HSS bits, extending their life by three times or more.

Trivia:

The Greek Titans give titanium its name, not Titania Queen of the Faeries. That means the American pronunciation Ty-tanium is the correct one.

†Titanium Nitride (TiN)

Titanium Aluminium Nitride (TiAlN)

This variant of Titanium Nitride extends bit life by over five times but is expensive and hard to get hold of.

Titanium Carbon Nitride (TiCN)

This is another hard, corrosion resistant coating for milling bits, better than standard TiN, though I can't find any exact figures. TiAlN and TiCN are also available in several colour appearances. It's caused by variations in the physical deposition process, cool for bike parts, jewellery etc., but irrelevant to us.

Polycrystalline Diamond (PCD) Bits

A 0.5mm layer of diamond particles sintered to a Tungsten Carbide base for drilling abrasive aluminium alloys and carbon reinforced plastics, not applicable here and hard to find.

Diamond & Zirconium Powder Coatings

Used for cutting tiles and other hard materials, not suitable for our purposes.

As with jewellery, zirconium is a cheaper alternative to the diamond. It's used for the same purposes and unsuitable for us.

Drill Accessories

When I put up a shelf in our en-suite bathroom by eye it worked... as long as you stand cylindrical objects on their base and not on their side. I'm not allowed to put up shelves any more...

You have binocular vision, you can keep a drill straight in one plane by looking down at it. But that doesn't work when it has to be perpendicular in all directions. Until we evolve at least one additional eye on a stalk, that's just the way it is.

Drill Guides

This simple platform with rotating sleeves is the answer. It keeps the drill bit perpendicular to the surface in every direction.

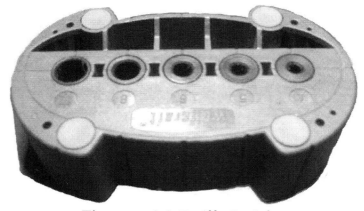
Figure 44 Drill Guide
†Drill Guide

Magnetic Clamp

You may wish to consider renting a magnetic clamp drill or a clamp for your existing drill, using them is self explanatory. Look at the bit from all angles before you start. While drilling it won't move around or get tired and you can focus on the pressure and using your free hand to lubricate the bit.

Bubble Gauge

An interesting alternative if the drill has to be **vertical** (as opposed to **perpendicular** to a surface which might not, itself, be horizontal) is to buy a small, self adhesive bull's eye level, put the drill in a vice and check it's vertical in all directions, then stick the bull's eye to the drill... if the drill is flat at the back it's an easy decision.

†Bubble Gauge

Screwdrivers & Driver Bits

Let's be clear, prevention is better than cure. A damaged screw head is almost always the result of camming-out of the head. This damages the opening, whether it's a simple slot or something more advanced.

There are several designs of bit tip designed to grip the inside of the head opening to prevent the tip spinning out. I've tried the Wera Kraftform Lasertip® screwdrivers and they are fantastic. You can feel the difference.

†Screwdriver Bits

†Screwdrivers

Air Duster

If you don't own a compressor, these things are a cheap, easy alternative. An aerosol can of compressed air, which usually comes with a tube to reach tricky areas.

†Air Dusters

Grinding Paste

This paste increases abrasion between surfaces. Elsewhere we covered screwdriver bits with diamond coating or laser etching to prevent camming-out. If you don't have those use this paste to achieve a similar effect using a standard bit.

†Grinding Paste

Lubricants

Cutting Lube

These come in a variety of viscosities. Some are liquids designed to pump into machinery, others are thick creams smeared into a bored hole as you drill. These are the most practical for use on a vehicle.

†Cutting Lubricants

Penetrating Lube

These have low surface tension to ease into tiny spaces. There are more details in the **Lubricating** section and links to some examples below.

†Penetrating Oils

Freeze Sprays

One of these was the key to freeing the worst stuck bolt I've come across so far, an Alfa rear brake calliper. Don't get me started. Again there are full details of how to use it in the **Freezing** section.

†Freeze Sprays

Big Guns

Sometimes a BFG is the only answer... not Big Friendly Giant in this context though... think Duke Nukem.

Power Tools

Power tools are our best ally once we reach the mid-point of our system. You don't need to buy all this stuff up front, wait for a situation where the low risk steps don't work. Pop to the shops or the internet and attack things afresh... you'll need a rest anyway at that point!

Power Sources

Tools all need a power source, they fall into three categories:

- ◆ Pneumatic (compressed air)
- ◆ Mains
- ◆ Cordless (battery powered)

Pneumatic

I don't expect many of us own a compressor which can drive power tools, but we can borrow or rent one.

Pros Of Air

The two principal advantages of compressed air tools are raw power and safety.

Not using electricity when working outside is an enormous benefit and you are often near flammable items, so that's another plus. Sparks from bits or blades are still a danger, so you're never off the hook about safety. There is a section dedicated to **Fire Suppression**.

Air tools are lighter and smaller because there's no motor or batteries inside and the pressures involved are huge, so they generate tremendous torque. Torque is available instantly for air and electric motors.

Cons of Air

The major downside of compressed air is the expense of buying, running and maintaining a full system. Low sales volumes mean the compressor and accessories are expensive. If you go air, go all air with impact wrenches, grinders, drills and saws because you might negotiate a discount.

Another minor kink, pun intended, is the hose which powers the tools is much bulkier than an electric cable. You also need to take care not to bend, crush, slit or otherwise damage them.

Mains

We aim this book at people doing DIY so we won't be dealing with three-phase here... that's for pros with a workshop and a dedicated power supply. We're talking about the standard supply at your house or in your shed, which varies with the country you're in. Our first concern is safety.

Trivia:

They invented the electric chair as a marketing stunt. Thomas Edison wanted to show Direct Current (DC) was safe. He invented the electric chair to show how dangerous Alternating Current (AC) is. He also electrocuted an elephant sentenced to death for killing three of its captors after one of them tried to feed it a lit cigarette. Horrific but true story... DC still lost.

Electrocution Protection

These devices go under an annoying variety of names depending on your country:

- Residual-Current Device (RCD)
- Residual-Current Circuit breaker (RCCB)
- Ground Fault Circuit Interrupter (GFCI)
- Ground Fault Interrupter (GFI)
- Appliance Leakage Current Interrupter (ALCI)

The key here is sensitivity and speed. These devices detect any imbalance in the current on the live and return (neutral) side of a circuit. If that is passing through you, you need a device which disconnects fast. Here in the UK this must be less than 40 milliseconds (0.04 seconds) and it should be similar everywhere else.

Do not buy a cheap knock-off, your life depends on it. You must investigate the correct markings for safety standards in your country, pay a sensible price and buy from a reputable outlet.

Frequencies and voltages vary from country to country, so it's too complex to cover here, check your local regs. With online buying take extra care, ensure the device is not for an unfamiliar environment.

†Electrocution Protection

Mains Pros

Mains operated equipment is cheap and plentiful.

The second factor is that you probably own an electric drill and at least one electric saw. Add an angle grinder and impact wrench, and you're ready for almost our entire bag of tricks.

Mains Cons

Mains tools are a splendid solution in the right conditions. Remember: we should use them with caution in wet or damp conditions, even with an RCD to protect you.

Electric motors are heavy and the mains ones used in power tools are large. You won't get the massive torque of the air powered tools with over 1200Nm (900 lb ft). DeWalt have an 18v cordless impact wrench called the XR, which didn't exist when I first wrote this book. The brushless motor generates 900Nm (660 lb ft), only 25% less than the air powered tool, so the gap is closing. A friend uses one for changing wheels on his track day car, it is a beast. Developments driven by electric vehicle (EV) development will make these the preferred choice, in fact we would argue that's the case already. Electric RPM tools like drills and oscillating saws are improving at the same time.

Cordless

The advantage of cordless tools is no cable or pipe getting in your way and there's no high voltage to deal with. They are the second most compact, after air powered, the only downside is the lower maximum torque compared to air. But we shouldn't need it, much of this book is about avoiding brute force of that kind.

It's sensible to buy a package with at least two batteries and a charger. A few companies are doing rapid charge systems which fill a battery in under an hour, so using one battery while another charges is a practical reality.

Cordless devices will get there with enough patience and batteries.

Drills (Borers)

Drilling is about progressive cutting, cumulative revolutions are the key to *ŧdrills*, not revolutions per minute, high revs just create heat. You need torque if using the drill to drive screws, bolts or large diameter bits. Buy the hardest, sharpest bits you can afford. Press without leaning your entire body into them, keep them cool and lubricated, and be patient.

Air Hammer/Chisel

Sometimes you cut off one side, or even both sides of a bolt through joined parts, and rust still holds the stump in place. A _†powered hammer/chisel_ or electric equivalent is like a hammer drill, but the tip doesn't rotate.

Impact Wrenches

You hear these gizmos whining and clattering in the background of all pro garages and Formula 1 pits. They're the most versatile and timesaving device a professional will use. It separates them from us mere mortals. There is light at the end of the tunnel... and it isn't an oncoming train.

Figure 45 Impact Wrenches

Air Impact Wrenches

Wikipedia say the torque of these ranges from 118Nm to 47,600Nm. Crikey, you'll need a mate to hang on to that second one! Make sure you can adjust the torque output, otherwise you could shear the shaft on your first attempt.

Mains Impact Wrenches

Mains operated impact wrenches seem to peak around 450Nm at the time of writing, above the lower end for the pneumatic ones, but nowhere near their maximum. This doesn't matter for domestic use, it's about vibration rather than brute force. We are trying to *avoid* shearing the thing, but crack and disrupt the brittle crystals causing the problem. You may hire professional 110v equipment, but remember you'll need a step-down transformer in some countries.

Cordless Impact Wrenches

†Impact Wrenches

Angle Grinders

If you absolutely, positively got to grind the m***********r off, accept no substitute. You'll need to extract the sawn off stump, but we've got that covered.

As with Impact Wrenches, these come in mains, cordless and pneumatic. The same arguments apply to size, cost and power. The prime feature is RPM rather than torque, though there is a correlation between the two because high RPM gives the spinning disc momentum. There's a third type using a high RPM fuelled motor like a chainsaw. They use these on building sites and they are too big for our purposes.

Figure 46 Angle Grinders

It is important to use the correct disc for the material you are grinding. Stainless steel, for instance, is very hard and can damage grinder discs or saw blades.

†Angle Grinders

Powered Belt Files

This doesn't have the brute power of a **Grinder,** but it is more precise. It's ideal for smoothing rounded shoulders from a damaged head or fastener and perfect for filing flats onto a protruding shaft.

Figure 47 Power Files

†Powered Belt Files

Saws

Saws are, like all the destructive tools, a last resort. But if cutting through an exposed section of a shaft frees the assembled parts, at least you can work on them on the bench.

Reciprocating Saws

Reciprocating saws mimic a normal sawing action, pushing and pulling the blade. The blade is shallower than the one in a hand saw, so you can cut gentle curves. These are okay for cutting a shaft, but the body stops you attacking a head close to a surface, for that we use an **Oscillating Saw** or a **Grinder**.

Oscillating Saws aka Multi-Tools

Oscillating saws (aka Multi-Tools) are the preferred option. These tools vibrate the blade sideways, like a hyperactive pendulum. The sharpened tip allows you to create cut outs in flat surfaces, approach a shaft or head from the side or access restricted spaces. The protruding arm means the bulky body is less of a problem.

†Multi-Tools (Oscillating Saws)

Big Levers

Breaker Bars

The methods in this book reduce the force needed to move a thread below the level where something breaks, this can still a big number. The simplest way is to apply a long lever.

Figure 48 Breaker Bars

Like Sockets, Breaker Bars come with square drives 1/4 inch, 3/8 inch, 1/2 inch, 3/4 inch and above. The bigger the drive, the longer the lever. If you only want two, start with 1/2 and 3/8 inch as they cover a wide range of socket sizes. The 1/4 inch fastener sizes rarely need immense force. Remember, this is the drive size... you can still use Metric sockets.

†Breaker Bar

Long Spanners

All the major brands offer long handled versions of their spanners. The vast majority are ring spanners, confirming our advice that Ring is King.

Figure 49 Long Spanners

†Long Spanners

Heat Sources

You will find many videos online showing how heat can free stubborn fasteners or shafts. We've delayed it to minimise risk because it's more hazardous than other methods. But heat has its place. The three principal ways to heat a piece of metal are:

◆ External heat from burning gas.
◆ Electric from current or arc.
◆ Induction, from fluctuating magnetic field.

†Heat Sources

Science Bit:

The mechanism is simple to understand - expansion. Expanding a ring with heat makes the hole inside get bigger. The shaft is heated by conduction, it's always cooler than the fastener and won't swell as much.

WARNING: For Best Results

For best results we should turn the fastener while still hot. Guess what I'm going to say next? Gloves, eye protection, water, fire blanket and fire extinguisher... OK? NEVER heat the fastener or shaft with the spanner in situ, you'll ruin the spanner. Remember the head, shaft and spanner will be hot for a considerable period afterwards.

External Heating

We need to heat things cherry red while trying to avoid getting them too much hotter than that. All these gases burn above the melting point of steel 1,370°C or 2,500°F so the full Oxyacetylene outfit is unnecessary if freeing things is your only goal. There are plenty of hand held DIY options with built in piezoelectric lighters. Conduction of heat from hot gas to the metal is not 100% efficient. We need a gas which burns a fair bit hotter than the melting point.

Butane : burns at 1,430°C (2,600°F) and doesn't melt steel. It will melt copper and aluminium. This seems ideal for us, but you'll be there a while and use a lot of gas. Something hotter used with care is a better choice.

Propane : is the next step up. It burns at 1,995°C or 3,623°F and was the professionals' choice until the invention of...

MAPP Propane : MAP Propane or MAPP burns at a staggering 2,925°C or 5,300°F. Now you see why I said you don't need Oxyacetylene at 3,500°C or 6,330°F. It's expensive and bulky. It's also much more dangerous. All for a gain you don't need unless you are cutting and welding. This lightweight regulator assembly will fit cylinders of various sizes. The cylinders should have a valve so you can remove them when not in use.

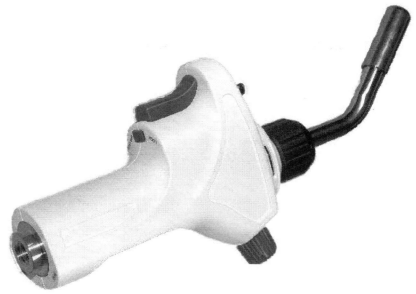
Figure 50 MAPP Burner

†MAPP Propane

Induction Heaters

WARNING: Electronics & Pacemakers
Do not use these near delicate electronic equipment as induced currents may cause damage. Disconnect the vehicle batteries and ECUs. If you or anyone nearby has a pacemaker, check the instructions about safe distance.

Wherever you can't use external heat, this may be your only option, if the coil will fit. While there are no naked flames, the fastener still gets hot. You must still take the usual precautions using equipment safe near high voltages.

There are only a few at present. They have dropped from four figure professional prices to half that. When starting a major project like a vehicle restoration, these are worth considering.

The big pro here is safety, unless you wear a pacemaker. They are much safer than external heating or arc welding. If you can't buy, consider renting one.

Science Bit:

Current flowing through a wire meets resistance, which dissipates some electrical energy as heat. The pulsing electromagnetic field inside the induction heater generates eddy currents (or Foucault currents) which heat it. We have an electric hob using this principle and which works well with cast iron cookware.

†Induction Heaters

Welders

WARNING: Electronics & Pacemakers
Do not use near delicate electronic equipment. Induced currents may cause damage. Disconnect the earth from batteries, consider disconnecting ECUs. Anyone nearby with a pacemaker must keep a safe distance as specified by the maker.

You can find more details on the Learn section of our website. Those of you who own one don't need the detail, those of you considering a purchase need only a quick outline. Allow time and material for plenty of practice...

Tip:
If untrained, you must attend a training course.
†Welding Books

In a nutshell, you are melting the junction of two materials so they merge. Without filler we call this an autogenous or fuse weld, the spot welds used on thin metal are a good example. All other welding adds a filler to add strength to the joint.

Metals oxidise in air and that process is faster when the metal is hot. The welded metal and the filler need protection. You can't operate in a vacuum like the filament of a bulb, so you need a different way to exclude the oxygen.

The inert gases used in gas shielded welding provide that shield. Good technique dictates you leave the gas running for a few seconds while the weld cools down.

In gasless systems we achieve oxygen exclusion with flux. The word derives from the Latin fluxus - flow. Sometime welding rods have flux coated on the outside, some down the middle. That makes little practical difference.

Some think the flux based systems are a little crude, as the flux can generate smoke and cause spatter. That can make the weld untidy, though easy to tidy up afterwards. The gas based systems, especially TIG, are the gold standard for X-Ray quality welds.

We can use TIG welders without filler for freeing rusty or damaged fasteners. They are an excellent localised heat source for a cleaned up head or nut. You can expand them to crack, crush and flake the rust seizing the fastener.

For snapped or sheared shafts, welding offers the chance to re-attach the original head. You can substitute a nut or rod by welding onto the stump. We can use the same trick for damaged heads, attaching a rod as a lever or welding on a nut bigger than the original head. In both cases, the expansion and contraction cycles help free the trapped shaft. In these cases a simple gasless welder with fluxed solder is adequate.

†Arc Welders

Chemicals
Dissolving is late in our suggested order of actions. Apparently a gentle solution compared to hammers, big levers and power tools, the problem here is practicality. Chemicals are messy, complex, and pose a hazard to the workpiece and the user.

†Cleaners

Home Brew
You can find recipes for exotic rust busting and thread loosening brews on the internet. Many involve Automatic Transmission Fluid (ATF) mixed with other things. All the chefs claim their brew works better than any off-the-shelf product. Why not? I'll tell you...

These brews are noxious, may not work, and you can't predict they're behaviour with other materials. The commercial solvents will:

- Work or give your money back.
- Declare hazards and any potential for collateral damage.
- Be less likely to cause a fire or generate poisonous fumes.

Trivia:

Cautionary Tale

A farmer friend of mine once mixed a weed killer with a fertiliser "To save time." The mixture gave off a green gas. I'm guessing might have been chlorine because some weed killers are chlorates. The resulting liquid ate through his friend's shoes. We can all learn from that.

There are many commercial products to clear whatever is stopping your fastener from moving. They may still melt your shoes, but at least they'll declare it in advance and they shouldn't behave like a chemical weapon as long as you follow the instructions.

Solvents for Rust

Can you save a few quid with simple household chemicals? This was going to be a section describing the use of vinegar to dissolve rust, one of the most popular bits of "common knowledge" doing the rounds. Looking for verification I found a problem, acetic acid reacts with steel to form rust. It reacts with the iron oxide too, but any steel that exposes just oxidises again in a never ending cycle. There are also videos of people proving this by leaving things in vinegar for weeks or months... they dissolve. Use a dedicated solvent to dissolve the oxide, leaving the metal intact.

†Solvents for Rust

Solvents for Oil (Degreasers)

A degreaser is a good first step in automotive applications. This may seem a little strange later when we lubricate everything again. But we're talking caked on, dried out stuff contaminated with dust and grit. This is acting as a barrier which will prevent penetrating lubricants from reaching the thread.

†Degreasers

Solvents for Paint (Strippers)

If the fastener is under a layer of paint, we need to remove that. As with grease, this allows the penetrating lubricants we apply to do their job. If it becomes necessary to use heat in later phases, it is also safer. There's less combustible material near the flame and you get noxious smoke. You should wear an appropriate mask.

†Paint Strippers

Nut Splitters

I'll avoid the obvious gags here and press straight on. You'll need at least two of these in different sizes to cover the most common sizes.

Figure 51 Nut Splitter

The frame goes over the shaft **and** nut, then you use a spanner to crank in the cutter until it fractures. Damage to the thread is a possibility, don't use this if re-use of the shaft is essential.

†Nut Splitters

Bolt Croppers

A bolt cropper comes in handy for tidying up if you are going to install fresh screws parallel to unusable ones. Use it to sever a shaft to free part of an assembly, remove heads, trim damaged thread, or tidy a jagged stump.

189

Figure 52 Bolt Croppers

The leveraging effect of the offset pivot points is visible in the photo. The handles are wide apart, but the jaws have only moved a small amount. It's our Work = Force x Distance equation again, see the **Six Simple Machines** appendix for a refresher.

Some countries prohibit stores from selling above a specified length to civilians. The larger versions can cut through hardened steel like chain links, handcuffs and padlock shackles.

†Bolt Croppers

Special Tools

Sometimes a mad inventor has experienced the same problem as you. They go to their shed, drink sherry and invent something ingenious. Don your curly wig, horn-rimmed spectacles and white lab coat for the world of Special Tools.

Screw Extractors

These fall into two categories, single ended and double ended. Both designs work with a drill or cordless screwdriver, extraction uses it in reverse.

The single-ended extractors are a standard 1/4" hex drive used for screwdriver bits. You can use any 1/4" handles but a T-shaped is the best choice or use the handle from a tap and die set. A socket handle with a 1/4" female drive on the back would also be an excellent choice. Rotate lefty loosey to extract...

Figure 53 Single Ended

These single-ended extractors are simple, resembling a cross-head screwdriver bit with sharpened edges to grip the opening on the screw, even when the sides are sloping because of damage. The shape is the same as the ***tapered reverse tap*** shown elsewhere. A left-handed helix pulls it into the hole, then reverses the screw out.

The procedure is simple. First fit the correct bit for the size of the screw. Lubricate the screw thread, put the drill-driver in its lowest gear, and select reverse. Squeeze the trigger gently to back the stump out slowly. This avoids shearing.

For a slot headed screw you must make a pilot hole. Unlike the double ended one's you'll need a separate drill bit, they will mark the size on the bit or the case it came in. Don't go too deep or you'll snap the head off the shaft, you need just enough to engage the extractor tip.

Figure 54 Double Ended

These look like double ended taps. In fact there's a stubby drill bit at one end, shown here on the left, and a conical reverse tap at the other. Pairing like this guarantees the pilot hole is the perfect diameter and depth.

Use the drill tip first, drilling clockwise to clear the damaged drive hole away, leaving a shallow hole. Don't go too deep, you'll drill to the shaft and snap the head off. Some designs have a depth stop collar, that's the best type to get.

Flip the bit around. Reverse the drill. Engage the tap in the hole from the first step, extract slowly as described before.

†*Screw Extractors*

Stud Extractors

No matter how careful we are, a head will shear away from a shaft or a shaft will shear close to its fastening assembly. The damage may already have been there, or you were overenthusiastic. That doesn't matter at this point.

Stud extractors are the tools used to extract sheared shafts. The term stud in this context is a threaded bar with no head on either end. They insert studs into threaded holes, then attach other pieces with nuts. A good example is older model engine blocks. The studs facilitate accurate location and alignment of the gaskets and cylinder head.

As with snapped heads, the techniques available depend on the amount of thread showing, with more options for a stump than snapped flush.

†*Stud Extractors*

Sheared Shaft Protruding

Without a head to use, we need a tool for gripping the headless shaft. Most involve squeezing the shaft in a way where lefty-loosey rotation squeezes even harder, with two designs working in either direction. Reverse taps act as a surrogate for the head. The section on **Snapped** has techniques for creating new surfaces to grip with basic tools.

Chuck Style Gripper

This looks like and works like a drill chuck. You place the jaws over the snapped off shaft and twist them shut. The operating shaft for closing the jaws is hexagonal on the outside, so you can use a long handled ring spanner. Inside the hexagon is a 1/2" square drive opening for an impact wrench, which is the better method if you own one.

Figure 55 Chuck Style Back

This is an excellent method. It's simple, quick, and uses vibration rather than brute force if used with the impact wrench. It applies force round the centre axis of the snapped shaft like an enlarged version of the original head.

Figure 56 Chuck Style Side
†Chuck Style

Self Clamping Socket

This cool gizmo works in both directions. So the Rock technique is doable with this and you can insert a new stud with it later. Some designs only work lefty-loosey for right-hand threads. Inside, three jaws grip in both directions. They grip harder as you apply more force.

Figure 57 Self Clamping Socket
†Clamp Style Sockets

Knurled Clamp

As you can see two different sized holes, with a hardened square drive cylinder set off centre. Put a stud or sheared shaft through the smallest one which fits.

Figure 58 Knurled Clamp Bottom

As you swing the cylinder, the off centre wheel swings onto the shaft and digs in. The harder you pull, the harder it digs in. Works clockwise, or anti-clockwise, applying force off centre, increasing leverage. You should always repeat cleaning and lubrication techniques to avoid another shear.

Figure 59 Knurled Clamp Top

†Knurled Clamps

Reverse Thread Socket

These look like standard sockets, inside they have a reversed (left hand) thread which narrows towards the driven bottom. We can lower this cone shaped thread over:

◆ a rounded off head

◆ a headless shaft

◆ a locking wheel nut

They tighten themselves on as you turn them lefty-loosen.

Figure 60 Reverse Thread Socket

Hardened like impact sockets, the internal thread can cut into smooth sided items like a locking wheel nut. The force needed to wind on the tapered thread increases until it's greater than the force needed to move the seized item. The only downside is extracting the stud from the socket afterwards.

Tip:

When I removed a set of locking nuts, I'd lost the key for I went over to a friend's workshop. He has a bench vice, and we used that to extract the item from the tapered thread each time. Leave the extractor on the breaker bar, clamp the item you've just removed in the vice jaws and wind out. Reverse thread: Righty loosey! It occurs to me now that lubricating the inside with some copper grease or other anti-seize might ease extracting the removed item from the socket.

†Reverse Thread Sockets

Sheared Shaft Flush

More difficult, but not: "Game over, man! Game over!" There's a non-destructive technique in this section. If that fails you can drill out the shaft and clear the thread with a Tap as described elsewhere. If that goes wrong you can drill a fresh hole then repair to the original diameter and pitch. We describe this in **Thread Replacement**.

Reverse Tapping

This is one of our options when the shaft snaps flush. We can also use it for the protruding stump mentioned in the previous section, but that carries the risk the shaft will split without support from the bore.

These tapered reverse thread taps are like the screw extractor, but larger. As before, you find the centre, punch a starter dent, drill a pilot hole the same size as the tip.

Figure 61 Tapered Reverse Tap

You can start it by tapping with a hammer, but remember tool steels are brittle. Turn anticlockwise until it bites and stops. Now you're transferring force into the shaft. All the drilling, hammering and movement of the shaft can help disrupt the rust bond. Like the others, reverse out manually or with a drill.

†Reverse Thread Taps

Taps & Dies

Drills are sharp at the tip and use the twisted channels around the shaft to remove waste from the hole, taps are for cutting a thread into that hole. They don't cut at the tip but use sharp, hardened, angled blades along the shaft. The grooves for the metal shavings (not shown above) run along, rather than around, the shaft.

†Taps & Dies

They make taps from hard but brittle tool steels. There's a risk of shearing one off in the pilot hole if you don't keep the tap aligned with the bore of the hole.

Cutting Threads

Most of us make this by hand. To make sure it's vertical, consider using a drill guide as described in **Accessories**. This will keep the tap perpendicular at the start, the most vital part of the process. Once you're in 1/2" (10mm), you can remove the tap and ditch the guide. Take care not to cross thread the tap when you put it back in.

Tip:

An excellent tip here is to go forwards half a turn, then back one quarter, to snap off the "tails" of swarf. Otherwise the tap can get jammed by the large curly bits of metal created by one continuous rotation. I'm a keen viewer of Forged in Fire and surprised when I see contestants who don't know this snap the tap off in their handle or pommel.

For thread clearance afterwards you should either use the taps with the short taper at the tip or the flat tipped ones. Always perform this by hand so you can feel the tap engaging with the thread. It should move without excessive force when not at the damaged threads. If it gums up, back it right out and clear the grooves.

Tip:

If you need a bush fix, you can use a bolt the same size and pitch as the thread to clear out debris. Place the bolt into a vice, grind several shallow slots down the length of the thread. Sand off any burrs, grease the slots and turn the bolt into the threaded hole. The grease picks up the dirt. If you're using thread-lock, the thread will require thorough degreasing.

Handles

The T-handle looks like a small drill chuck with a bar stuck through the top of the shaft. It's okay for smaller threads where you don't need both hands to turn the cutter. For larger threads there's more friction and they require more effort. We may need a bar type tap wrench with a two handed grip... best to have one of each.

Tap

As you can see taps are like drills with fine twists. The illustration is of tapered reverse twist taps used for extracting snapped off shafts. They also come with parallel sides and a tapered tip to assist "run in," or parallel along their entire length with a flat tip.

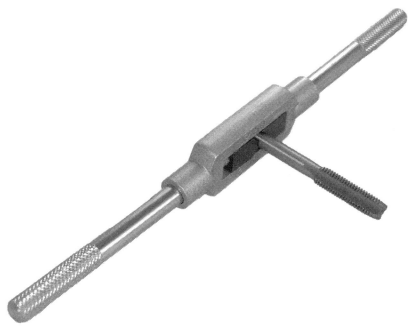

Figure 62 Taps

If you buy a complete set instead of a kit for one specific size look for useful additions like these. The small L-handle is for the smaller diameter taps where the hefty T-handle might snap them. The other item which looks like a comb with broken teeth is a thread gauge so you can determine the correct pitch to use. Engage the teeth using an undamaged part of the thread in the hole or on the damaged bolt.

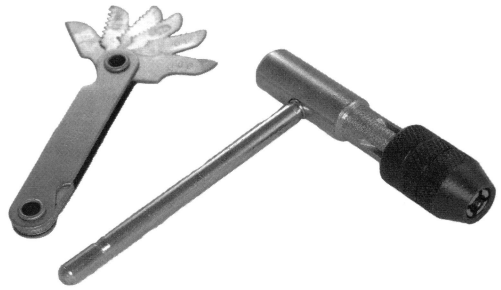

Figure 63 L-Handle & Gauge

†Taps

Die

Taps often come with matched dies, disc shaped tools with cutting blades inside. They cut external threads into plain bars for scratch-building your own shafts. Like taps, they have gaps for swarf.

Figure 64 Dies

Taps come in sets, in thread repair kits or on their own because drilling out snapped shafts is common. Sets of dies usually come with matching taps as part of a full set.

B: Time Saving Gadgets

These are things I left out of the Bare Essentials section because they aren't essential. But if you can afford them, you won't regret having any of these to hand when the need arises.

Thread Gauge

These are useful for measuring a removed but damaged fastener so you can buy a replacement or the correct diameter and pitch of thread repair coil. Also useful if you drilled out a shaft and want to use a tap to clear remnants of the thread. That assumes there's a fragment of the sheared bolt to measure, otherwise you'll have to use trial and error, make sure you turn the test bolt at least twice.

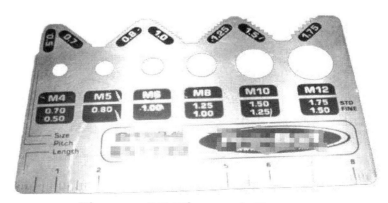

Figure 65 Thread Gauge

This one is metric. The v-shaped notches with teeth fit into the threads giving you the pitch, the distance a shaft moves per full rotation. The smaller that distance, the finer the thread, a 1.25mm is a finer thread than 1.5mm.

Using the holes is obvious, they give you the shaft diameter, for the metric system that's the size i.e. 12mm is M12. You can see STD and FINE pitches marked under the bolt sizes. There are exceptions, like an M12 bolt with a 1.25mm thread we found on an Alfa.

†Thread Gauge

Magnetic Torch
The LED has revolutionised the utility of portable lighting. Low power consumption means smaller batteries and longer burn time. They are much brighter than bulbs many times the wattage and they are cheap. That's an amazing set of benefits from one invention.

Figure 66 Magnetic Torch Front

Flexible shafts, hooks and magnets abound. But now it will run for 20 or 30 hours on one set of batteries and won't blow if it gets dropped.

†Magnetic Torch

Magnetic Oddment Holder

I only put this in as an excuse to use the word oddment... they are useful though.

Figure 67 Magnetic Oddment Holder Back

This one clips over your belt. There are also wrist versions and magnetic bowls you stick to the thing you are working on.

†Magnetic Oddment Holder

Flexible LED Mirror

These aren't the height of technology, it's a mirror on a ball joint at the end of a telescopic pole. It lets you look into places you can't stick your head at a fraction of the cost of a borescope camera, though they too are cheap now. Mine has a built in LED illuminator and I wonder how I ever did without one.

Figure 68 Flexible LED Mirror

†Flexible LED Mirror

LED Telescopic Magnet

These are just as handy for retrieving dropped tools as they are for dropped fasteners. Like the **Flexible LED Mirror,** I have an LED illuminated version of this. It will lift about a kilogram... fixed magnet, no batteries, amazing.

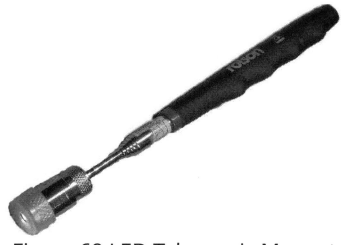

Figure 69 LED Telescopic Magnet

†*LED Telescopic Magnet*

Claw Retriever

Retrieving non-magnetic items, or ones too heavy for a small Magnetic Retriever, this may get the job done. It bears a spooky resemblance to a small Dalek gun, or, for fans of the B-Movie *Tremors*... a Graboid's mouth!

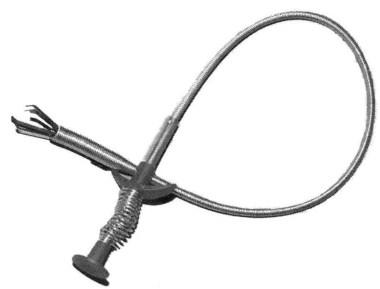

Figure 70 Claw Retriever

†*Claw Retriever*

C: PPE No Need to Bleed

This may seem an odd thing to include here, but there are good reasons to invest in a few items of purpose-designed clothing: safety and comfort. I'm puzzled why people get so angry at attempts to keep them safe if it causes even a small amount of inconvenience. Being comfortable means you can focus on the task, without distraction from being too hot, too cold, wet or in pain.

Safety Shmafety - No!

Skip the warnings go to *Clothing on page 213*

This isn't just about me covering my arse, but about you keeping yourself in one piece. Discipline about safety isn't weakness, it's strength. Unless you're in the Yakuza, there's no credibility in having missing fingers.

WARNING: Eyes

Please wear eye protection appropriate for the task, you know how uncomfortable even a speck of foreign material in your eye is. Given the crystalline nature of metal compounds, they have sharp edges and are something you don't want anywhere near your eyes.

WARNING: Ears

Some later techniques use power tools like impact wrenches which generate considerable

noise and you are close to it. I have tinnitus from one loud birthday party... it's a ruddy nuisance. You can buy a bag of †*memory foam earplugs* for less than the price of a pint, so please buy and use them.

WARNING: Skin

Gloves fall into several categories from thin synthetic gloves through padded and even fireproof. The thin gloves protect you from irritants while maintaining a good feel for objects and tools, padded gloves sacrifice tactility to protect you from knocks and scrapes. Tasks involving blow lamps or welding equipment need specialist gloves to protect you from the extreme temperatures involved. For mundane tasks use a barrier cream as a bare minimum. For brush on or spray chemicals, always follow the manufacturer's instructions regarding ventilation and other protection and take the container with you when seeking medical help.

WARNING: Lungs

There are a variety of different masks to protect you from dust, volatile vapours and even poisonous gas. Read the label and buy protection appropriate to the hazard.

WARNING: Fire/Heat

There are a variety of small handheld extinguishers you can keep handy when using extreme heat techniques. Remember, they use ingredients suitable for specific types of fire and unsuited to others. We deal with this under *Fire Suppression*.

WARNING: Electricity

Working with power tools outside or in a damp building, protect yourself from shorts. Shorts of the electrical kind, not the "should I wear Hawaiian board shorts over the age of forty" variety.

WARNING: Jacking

It bears repeating that changing a tyre at the roadside using only a jack is a calculated risk. Carrying out extensive work under a jacked up, otherwise unsupported car is inviting serious injury or even death.

Clothing

Clothing can protect you from everything from weather to impact injuries. Being comfortable and as safe as you can be means you can concentrate on the job.

Overalls

Overalls are a sensible, inexpensive investment. They stop you messing up your street clothes and don't have a gap to let in dirt and drafts. They don't require a belt, so there's no buckle to scratch or foul on things. Last, but not least, they don't exhibit your arse crack to everybody in the vicinity.

†Overalls

Gloves

Impact Gloves

The primary reason I bought a pair of these was my dislike of pain. When a tool loses its grip, some part of your hand always hits some nearby structure. The ribs and padding on these give you some protection.

Figure 71 Mechanix Gloves

The edges of some tools, spanners for instance, can be painful if you lean on them hard. But I type for a living, so maybe it's just me. Anyway, I find these grant me the confidence to pull or push harder.

The only downside of the padding is a slight lack of feel for delicate operations. Some gloves attempt to solve this with thin areas at the fingertips, but given delicacy and brute force rarely coincide, the simplest solution may be to take them off.

As with eye protection, you need specialist gloves for welding.
†Gloves

Trousers
All work trousers bristle with pockets and tool loops but these aren't always useful if you need to lie down and roll about. The ones with

envelope pockets hung from the waistband remain more upright when sitting or crouching, so the contents don't fall out.

Double stitching and doubling up of the material in high wear areas like knees and elbows are also common. This increases comfort and extends the useful life of the garment. Another excellent argument for using clothing designed to take a bit of punishment. Inverted pockets at the knees are for the insertion of knee pads, I haven't tried them myself... How the heck do they stay in there?

†Trousers

Shoes
I grew up in an era when these things were large, heavy and uncomfortable. Now they are lighter and feel like trainers. Ensure they conform to ISO 20345:2004 or the equivalent for your country. Too complex a subject for this book, but the Wikipedia page on this is excellent.

†Footwear

Hats
They can keep you warm when it's cold, dry when it's wet and shady when it's bright, and there's always the classic hard hat. They also keep at least some crap out of your hair.

†Hats

Eye Protection

I'll be honest here and admit I forget this the vast majority of the time. If I'm using a grinder, a file or even a drill, stuff with sparks and obvious sharp swarf I don't always remember. Tinkering with the car, I didn't bother; that was a mistake. One I aim to rectify.

†Eye Protection

Safety Glasses

There are several options here. You can buy the ones we all wore in the lab at school or the ones which look like super cool fashion items. The key is to suit the item to the task.

Figure 72 Safety Glasses

You need to ensure fine dust can't blow inside whatever you're wearing and with hot splinters, that they can't burn **through** the lenses.

†Safety Glasses

Safety Goggles

Use safety goggles rather than glasses when there's dust you don't want creeping past the gaps.

Figure 73 Safety Goggles
†Safety Goggles

Welding Masks

You must always use a welding mask, the same UV light which gives you a tan can do extreme and permanent damage to your eyes. Photokeratitis (aka arc eye) is sunburn of the cornea and conjunctiva at the corners of your eyes. Like sunburn you don't notice until several hours after exposure. Symptoms are watery eyes and a painful gritty feeling, like sand.

Science Bit:

Your closeness to the source of the UV is a large part of the problem. The intensity of all electromagnetic radiation decreases as the square of the distance. At one unit of distance it's one, at two it's a quarter, at four a sixteenth, etc. But the reverse applies to the rise as you get closer, move your face from four feet to one and the UV is sixteen times more intense.

†Welding Masks

Skin Protection

Barrier Creams

Take your pick between these and thin gloves, or switch between the two depending on the delicacy of feel you need for the task. Also, a complement to impact protecting gloves if they have no membrane.

†Barrier Creams

Nitrile Gloves

You can sacrifice top-level warmth or trauma protection for tactility by making the materials thinner. They are thin enough to wear under the *Impact Gloves* mentioned earlier. They've replaced allergenic powdered latex gloves with powder-less nitrile, in a variety of colours from Dexter purple to the standard serial killer black.

Figure 74 †Nitrile Gloves

Hand Cleansers

The chemicals used to lubricate, degrease, clean, strip and free things are often irritants. Some may even be under discussion as potential carcinogens with frequent or prolonged exposure. Gloves and barrier creams are a wise precaution. A good cleanser with a moisturiser to stop your skin cracking is also wise. Open sores are a serious threat to health. It isn't a silly affectation, it's essential.

†Hand Cleansers

Arc Tan

Arc tan isn't only a reference to a trigonometry function, it's the skin equivalent of photokeratitis and carries its own special risks. The intense bursts of ultraviolet (UV) light from welding are more intense than sunlight because you are close to it: yes, you can get "sunburn"... and skin cancer.

You should take the same precautions against permanent tissue damage as for strong sunlight. If you prefer to operate with your arms exposed because of the intense heat of the process, wear sunblock. You could use standard water based suntan lotion. Better still, look for a water based non-flammable Barrier Cream with UV block.

Respiratory Protection
These make you look like you've escaped from Walter White's meth lab, but some chemicals you'll be using are volatile and unpleasant, it's better to be safe than sorry.

†Respiratory Protection

Fire Suppression

I know this may seem like overkill now. It won't seem so paranoid when you are running in and out of your kitchen with jugs of water. Cars need fuel. Neither petrol nor diesel are as easy to light with a match as they are in the movies. But your car has high and low voltage electricity. For the latter parts of our process, where you are using a blow-lamp, they are essential. Be prepared... I'm sure I've heard that somewhere before...

†Fire Suppression

Fire Classes

It's important to understand fire classes for the UK, these are:

- ◆ Class A: general waste wood, paper, fabric, plastic
- ◆ Class B: flammable liquids petrol, diesel, paraffin
- ◆ Class C: flammable gas propane, butane
- ◆ Class D: burning metals magnesium, aluminium etc.
- ◆ Class E: fires involving electricity.
- ◆ Class F: Oil fires cooking oils and fats.

They don't classify electrical fires in Europe, it's based on the material you are extinguishing and electricity doesn't combust. Read the label and don't use conducting extinguisher mediums if the fire involves electricity.

Stick with gases, dry powders and AFFF (Aqueous Film Forming Foam). Check the manufacturer guidelines conductivity rating in kilovolts (kV) and safe use distance. AFFFs are okay for vehicular use as they do less damage to a running engine and leave far less residue. They use them a lot at motor sport events for this reason.

Fire Extinguishers Handheld

These are great because you can use them one handed... very useful if your other hand is on fire. A quick and dirty solution aimed at being close at hand. Don't misunderstand, these are potent little beasties.

They sent me on a fire course and I used one to put out a flaming oil tray single handed, in both senses. They've banned the old BCF extinguishers like the one I used, but I'm sure the greener equivalent is as good, if not better.

†Handheld Extinguishers

Fire Extinguishers Medium

These are best used with both hands, but are still lighter than the full sized ones you see in offices. They provide a much longer burst than the hand held ones.

†Medium Sized Extinguishers

Fire Blankets

This is a sensible investment, it can smother a fire or when placed between the heat source and the flammable stuff, prevent one.

†Fire Blankets

D: The Six Simple Machines + Hydraulics

Force/Distance Trade Off

The mathematics uses a simple equation:

$$\textit{Work or Energy in Joules(J)} = \textit{Force x Distance}$$

You can see the roots of several Force versus Distance trade-offs.

Fixed Work

Power (Watts) is Work per Second (J/s). Your leg muscles have an upper limit on Force and Power, so we use gears.

Low gears spin your legs through many revolutions, a long Distance, but with low Force. High gears decrease the revs and shorten the distance, but you push harder.

Fixed Force

Sometimes the Force you can use is limited, but you can increase the Distance to do more Work for that maximum effort.

Example: Your body weight limits a manual pulley system. With one pulley there's a 1:1 balance, if you are lighter than the load it won't move. Two pulleys double the force and halve the distance.

Fixed Distance

When space limits movement, we fix Distance. This means the only option is to multiply Force to produce the desired Work.

Without vacuum assistance a car brake pedal only has an inch or two of space to move. The calliper pistons only move a fraction of that. You have two Force x Distance equations for the same Work, excluding losses. Force multiplies by differences in the surface area of the piston at the pedal (Master) and the brake disc (Slave).

Mechanical Advantage

Understanding The **Six Simple Machines** will help you in three ways:

- ◆ How threads, work.
- ◆ How tools multiply muscle force.
- ◆ How to create your own solutions.

Trivia:

Things don't become more or less true with age, but these discoveries are old, defined during the Renaissance, the 14th to 17th centuries.

A simple machine applies a force to change the direction or magnitude of another force. It's the second part which interests us - magnitude. These examples show mechanical advantage multiplying the forces you apply to objects and fasteners.

This isn't just about tools multiplying force to move a fastener, but fasteners multiplying force to hold parts together. For example, a screw is a shallow, inclined plane (ramp) around a shaft. Long rotational movements translate to tiny movements of the shaft or fastener which exert sizeable forces. Double your force with the tool and triple it with the screw and the result is: F x 2 x 3 = 6 times the force.

Lever

A lever is ***a beam or rigid rod pivoted around a hinge or fulcrum*** like a crowbar under a paving slab. The shallow bend and the ground or adjacent slab work as the fulcrum.

The word lever, pronounced lu-vay, originates from a French verb meaning "to raise."

The relative position of the fulcrum determines the mechanical advantage. Let's start with a simple but exceptional case: a children's seesaw, the same length on either side. We calculate mechanical advantage by dividing the length on the short side into the long one. If they are equal the answer is one, there's no advantage, two people of equal weight will balance.

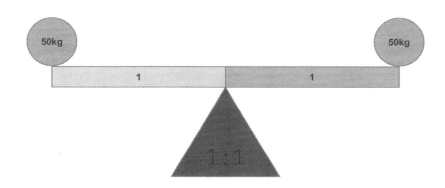

In the second example, the fulcrum is off centre. One side is two units, the other is one. Pressing on the long end gives a mechanical advantage ratio of two. The amount of force needed to balance 100kg on the shortest end will be 50kg at the longer end. Force and mass correlate because gravity is the same on both sides.

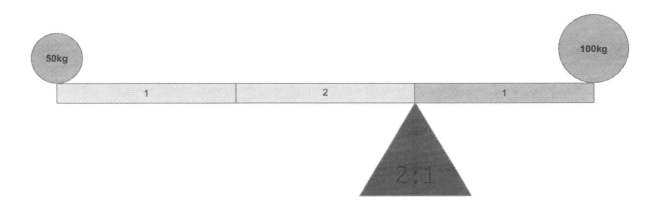

Wheel & Axle

In this context we attach the wheel to the axle so they move together as a single piece around a shaft or bearing, like a round door handle.

We can drive wheels at the rim or by the axle, mechanical advantage is opposite in these two cases.

A simple example of rim drive is a pipeline valve which uses a circular handle to open and close, the bigger the wheel, the easier the twist.

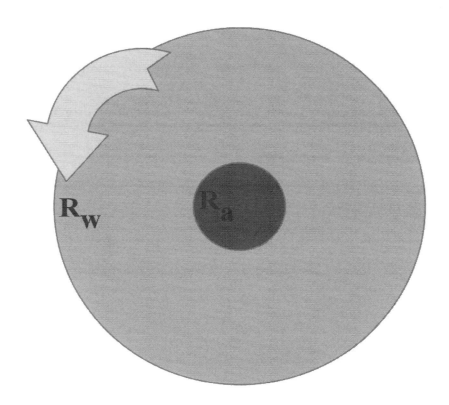

The mechanical advantage of a wheel is proportional to the difference in radius between the axle Ra and the wheel Rw: **Rw/Ra**

Drive a winch from the axle, not as a geared pulley, and the bigger the cylinder, the harder it is to lift the load. This increases as the winch cord increases the drum size.

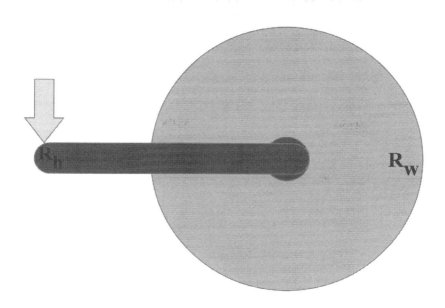

Trivia:

Cars are the same, the mechanical advantage is against you. That's why the 850cc engine Issigonis Minis were so nippy... they only had 10" wheels. Your Range Rover is slower because of those 24" spinners.

Pulley

A pulley is a Wheel & Axle designed to support and redirect a rope, cable, chain or belt.

The assembly of the wheel, axle and the frame with anchor points, is a block. A block can have multiple wheels rotating around the same axle, not attached to it. That's why we call it a spindle instead. To save space, these are the most common type of pulley.

For our explanations, imagine a sequence of single pulleys. We'll assume ideal parallel ropes with no frictional losses.

Mechanical advantage in pulley systems derives from the number of cords pulling up on the load. They divide the input force. Fixed pulleys change the direction but confer no mechanical advantage. W here is Weight, not Work.

The edge case of a single fixed overhead pulley lifting weight **W** requires the force of **W** to balance. Like a children's Seesaw.

Here the movable pulley attaches to the ceiling on one side. The pulley is dangling, attached to **W** and we pull the tail of the rope upwards, tension drops to **W/2**.

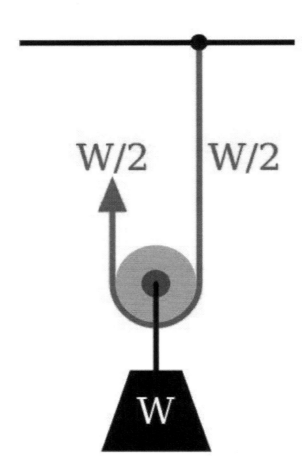

A simple two pulley system, anchored to the ceiling at the first pulley, anchored at the far end. The second pulley lifts W by its attachment point. This needs an input force, or tension, of W/2 to balance.

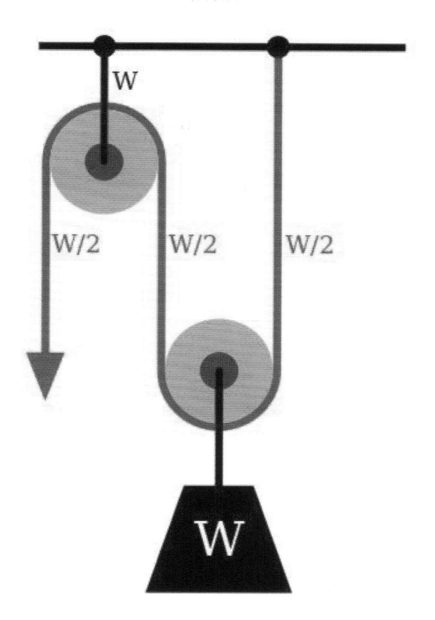

W

W/2   W/2   W/2

W

A three pulley system with **W** attached to pulley two and the end of the rope has tension of **W/3**. In practice you use even numbers of pulleys so you're always pulling downwards. It's unusual to attach the load to the rope, they typically attach it to a dangling block by a hook, or eye on the casing.

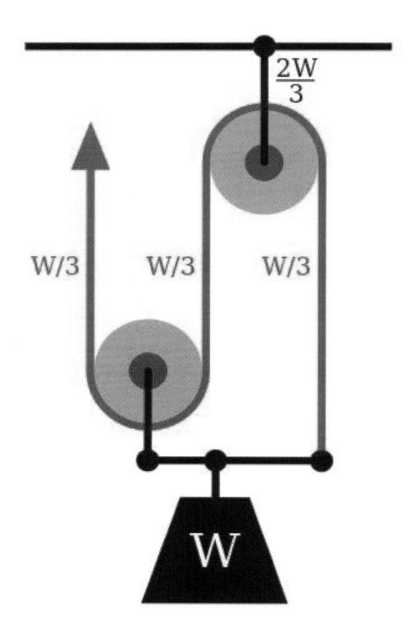

Cranes and marine rigging are two familiar contexts for the use of pulley systems.

Inclined Plane (Ramp)

An inclined plane is a straight trade-off of force and distance, lifting a weight against the force of gravity requires energy (work).

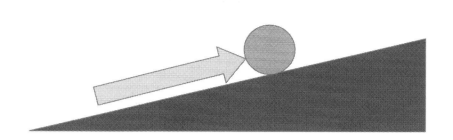

A ramp or gradient lets you lift an item using a smaller force over a larger distance. A 1:10 ramp goes forward ten metres, to go up one. This decreases the force by a tenth, excluding friction.

Inclined roads, wheelchair ramps and multi-story car parks are commonplace examples.

Wedge

Wedges are used to separate two objects or to split an object into two pieces. You can see the logical link to the Inclined Plane, the wedge is a portable, often hand held, version.

A wedge converts force applied to the blunt end to a force perpendicular (at 90 degrees) to it.

As with a ramp, the ratio will be length versus thickness. Wedges rely on the repeated application of a large force to move a small distance. Friction is much greater because both sides are in direct contact with surfaces they are trying to squeeze past.

Chisels use the wedge principle. A special case there is the use of wooden wedges in the quarrying and lumber industries. Once hammered in we soak them in water to make them swell. This splits the target over a period of hours or days. As water expands when it freezes, it's even more effective in Winter. The mechanical advantage multiplies when using more wedges, rather than larger forces.

Door stops are the most commonplace example. They turn sideways force from a sprung door 90 degrees onto the floor, so friction keeps the door open.

Screw

A screw converts rotary motion into linear motion and a torsional force to a linear one. In terms of the other simple machines, you can view it as a shallow Inclined Plane wrapped around a cylinder. The load is along the axis of the shaft.

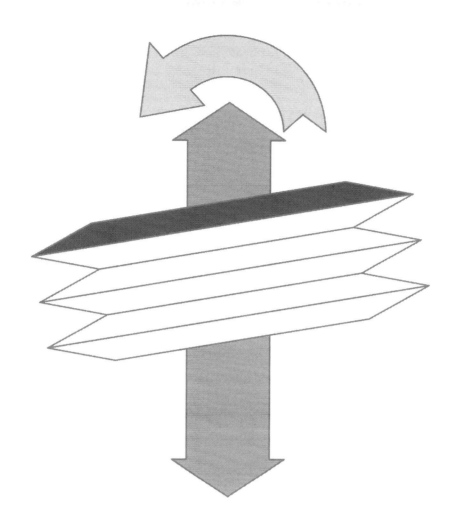

We gain mechanical advantage by altering the pitch. Pitch is the amount the shaft moves for each full rotation. Shallower threads make the plane longer, increasing mechanical advantage. Just like our bicycle example the long rotational distance with small force yields a shorter movement with a larger force. That balances the same **Work = Force x Distance** equation as the gears and Inclined Plane. The strength of a screw thread is also its weakness. Expose a long thread to something like cement and it's extremely hard to move by brute force alone.

Commonplace examples are many: nuts, bolts, screw jacks, cider presses, vices, wood screws, and corkscrews.

Hydraulics

Hydraulics aren't in the six simple machines, but I've included them for interest. From the "Jaws of life" used by rescue crews, to car jacks and brakes, hydraulics are a valuable tool.

Focused Force

Let's talk high heels and light tanks. We are used to pressure and most of us know standard atmospheric pressure at sea level is about 15 pounds per square inch (PSI). The unit shows pressure is *force per unit of area*. The pressure on each square inch in adjacent squares is the same, but the *total* force on a 3 x 3 grid is 9 times 15 pounds... 135 pounds! That multiplying effect is how hydraulic assistance works.

We can use the same principle to spread pressure from a fixed weight, to prevent damage and improve stability on soft surfaces. During the Falklands war British troops had to cross swamps, but they didn't go on foot, they used tanks. The lightweight Scorpion, with troops and gear all over it, exerts less force per unit of area than a booted foot, because of the vast area of the tracks.

Master/Slave Cylinders

You won't be at all surprised that hydraulics trade force and distance. They do this using pistons with differing surface areas. For the same volume of liquid pushed into a cylinder, the narrow one will move further than the wide one.

Imagine two syringes connected. You can push on either piston to move the other. The narrow one is easy to push and moves a long way. The wide one will move a short distance but produce greater force, because the pressure is equal over the inside of the both syringes and the pipe. The piston with the biggest area multiplies the *total* force, but moves a shorter distance.

I'm ignoring vacuum assistance in this example. Your car brakes use a small master cylinder moving several inches to press the small cylinders behind the brake pads a small amount with substantial force. We call these master (pedal) and slave (brake pad) cylinders.

OTHER BOOKS FROM NRTFM

The EDC Bible: Foundation

The EDC Bible 1: All Day Carry (ADC)
†*http://books2read.com/EDCBAllDayCarry*

The EDC Bible 2: Flexible Loadouts
†*http://books2read.com/EDCBFlexibleLoadouts*

The EDC Bible 3: Optimal Carry
†*http://books2read.com/EDCBOptimalCarry*

Fall Asleep in 60 Seconds Gadget Edition

- ◆ Trouble falling asleep?
- ◆ Keep waking up?
- ◆ Tired in the mornings? Bad Tempered?

   You may be suffering sleep poverty. I had the same problem and needed a solution. I am happy to share what I found

- ◆ A Simple, complete, drug free solution
- ◆ ... and gadgets to assist

   †http://books2read.com/FallAsleepIn60SecondsGadgetEdition

PLEASE LEAVE A REVIEW

We're a tiny independent publisher.
The Industry is dominated by giants.
Please help us stand out.
Most people won't buy things with no reviews.
If you haven't left one already, please leave a review!

This will take you to your preferred store:
†https://books2read.com/TheRustyNutBible

STAY IN THE LOOP

Advanced Review Copy List

If you want to help out and get free books in return, you can join our ARC team. ARC = Advance Reading Copy. Basically an early draft of the book for you to read and comment on if you wish to. You are not obliged to buy the book or review it when it comes out, but it would be great if you chose to. You'll get to see the finished product you helped create.

†Join our ARC Team!

Launch Discount List

If that seems a bit much, how about a sneaky heads-up for a huge discount at book launches?

†Join the Launch Discount List!

ACKNOWLEDGEMENTS

The author is not a representative of any brands mentioned. This book relies on the principle of nominative fair use. He acknowledges the true ownership of any and all trademarks referred to in the text.

I'd like to thank my wife Sooz for her continued patience regarding my new career. Thanks also to all my beta readers for spending hundreds of hours proofreading my stuff. Any remaining errors are my cat walking across the keyboard after the corrections :-)

IMAGE ATTRIBUTION

Below are links and license details for all the images I have used in this book not created by me. I have tried to use material which is free to use as I can't afford royalty fees at this stage in my career. If I have broken the terms of a licence, please get in touch with me and I'll correct it.

DISCLAIMER

Every effort has been made to ensure the research distilled into this book is correct, safe and current. We are covering a vast array of topics and mistakes can happen. We are also giving you the bare bones - to let you know the issues and give you coverage on unfamiliar subjects so you can expand your knowledge where needed.

If professionals in a speciality contradict this book, follow their lead. If you do things yourself you accept responsibility for problems caused by any lack of additional knowledge or training on your part.

If you find an error or omission please remember we're a small company. The call to your lawyer will cost you more than I earn in a week, you may be better off just emailing me for a correction :-)

You can contact me at: *tnrtfm.com*

ALLI

Proud Member
The Alliance of Independent Authors
†*Find out more*

THE END

Thank you for buying our book. If you bought it to solve a specific problem please visit *†TheRustyNutBible.com* and let us know how it went. We live in a culture which is too willing to discard and replace things which aren't truly broken. Repair and refurbishment take time and effort, but can be very rewarding. I hope the techniques and tools here help you save money and give new life to some useful, valued or beloved thing.

Cheers, Chas & Sooz

The End!

Printed in Great Britain
by Amazon